Ian McEwan's
Enduring Love

CONTINUUM CONTEMPORARIES

Also available in this series:

Pat Barker's *Regeneration,* by Karin Westman
Kazuo Ishiguro's *The Remains of the Day,* by Adam Parkes
Carol Shields's *The Stone Diaries,* by Abby Werlock
J. K. Rowling's *Harry Potter* Novels, by Philip Nel
Jane Smiley's *A Thousand Acres,* by Susan Farrell
Barbara Kingsolver's *The Poisonwood Bible,* by Linda Wagner-Martin
Irvine Welsh's *Trainspotting,* by Robert Morace
Donna Tartt's *The Secret History,* by Tracy Hargreaves
Toni Morrison's *Paradise,* by Kelly Reames
Don DeLillo's *Underworld,* by John Duvall
Annie Proulx's *The Shipping News,* by Aliki Varvogli
Graham Swift's *Last Orders,* by Pamela Cooper
Bret Easton Ellis's *American Psycho,* by Julian Murphet
Haruki Murakami's *The Wind-up Bird Chronicle,* by Matthew Strecher
Ian Rankin's *Black and Blue,* by Gill Plain
Michael Ondaatje's *The English Patient,* by John Bolland
Cormac McCarthy's *All the Pretty Horses,* by Stephen Tatum
Iain Banks's *Complicity,* by Cairns Craig
A.S. Byatt's *Possession,* by Catherine Burgass
David Guterson's *Snow Falling on Cedars,* by Jennifer Haytock
Helen Fielding's *Bridget Jones' Diary,* by Imelda Whelehan
Sebastian Faulks's *Birdsong,* by Pat Wheeler
Kate Atkinson's *Behind the Scenes at the Museum,* by Emma Parker
Hanif Kureishi's *The Buddha of Suburbia,* by Nahem Yousaf
Nick Hornby's *High Fidelity,* by Joanne Knowles
Zadie Smith's *White Teeth,* by Claire Squires
Arundhati Roy's *The God of Small Things,* by Julie Mullaney
Alan Warner's *Morvern Callar,* by Sophy Dale
Margaret Atwood's *Alias Grace,* by Gina Wisker
Vikram Seth's *A Suitable Boy,* by Angela Atkins

Forthcoming in this series:

Gabriel Garcia Marquez's *Love in the Time of Cholera,* by Tom Fahy
Philip Pullman's *His Dark Materials* Trilogy, by Claire Squires
Don DeLillo's *White Noise,* by Leonard Orr
Michael Cunningham's *The Hours,* by Tory Young
Jonathan Coe's *What a Carve Up!,* by Pamela Thurschwell
David Foster Wallace's *Infinite Jest,* by Stephen Burn

· IAN McEWAN'S

Enduring
Love

A READER'S GUIDE

ROGER CLARK
and
ANDY GORDON

CONTINUUM | NEW YORK | LONDON

2003

The Continuum International Publishing Group Inc
370 Lexington Avenue, New York, NY 10017

The Continuum International Publishing Group Ltd
The Tower Building, 11 York Road, London SE1 7NX

www.continuumbooks.com

Printed in the United States of America

Library of Congress Cataloging-in-Publication Data

Clark, Roger, 1950–
    Ian McEwan's Enduring love : a reader's guide / Roger Clark and
Andy Gordon.
        p.   cm. — (Continuum contemporaries)
    ISBN 0-8264-1478-8 (pbk. : alk. paper)
    1. McEwan, Ian. Enduring love.   I. Gordon, Andy, 1956–   II.
Title.   III. Series.
PR6063.C4E5333   2003
823'.914—dc21   2003003729

ISBN 0-8264-1478-8

Contents

1.

The Novelist   7

2.

The Novel   26

3.

The Novel's Reception   58

4.

The Novel's Performance   64

5.

Further Reading and Discussion Questions   85

The Novelist

In 1983 the leading literary periodical *Granta* published a number that showcased the twenty writers its editors described as the "Best of Young British Novelists." Although this seemed like an early example of the "listmania" that currently drives so much media discussion of the arts (*Granta* has repeated the exercise at ten yearly intervals), in hindsight it was an impressively accurate piece of prediction. The 1983 list could be used as a *Who's Who* of the late-twentieth-century British novel, including as it does such current luminaries as Martin Amis, Pat Barker, William Boyd, Salman Rushdie, Graham Swift and Rose Tremain. Prominent amongst the *Granta* nominees for future literary fame was Ian McEwan, who had already startled the literary world with two disturbing collections of short stories and two equally challenging novels. Twenty years on, he has established himself as one of the major writers of his time, receiving critical and popular acclaim for his remarkable body of work. McEwan's success stems, perhaps, from the way his fiction traces the arc of late-twentieth-century British history and culture whilst exploring the most personal levels of human experience.

Ian Russell McEwan was born in Aldershot on June 21, 1948. His father was a Regimental Sergeant-Major in the British army and was regularly posted abroad. As a result McEwan traveled widely as a child (or "army brat" as he has described himself), living mainly in Singapore and Tripoli. His mother had two children from a previous marriage but they were considerably older than McEwan so he felt himself to be "psychologically, an only child"—something he wrote about at greater length in a 1982 *Observer* article entitled "An Only Childhood." His father was, in McEwan's terms, a "kindly" but "domineering" man who imposed his will on his mother, Rose, about whom he has written a moving memoir. In this piece, entitled "Mother Tongue—A Memoir," first published in *The Guardian* (October 13, 2001) and now collected in a recent study of modern British fiction edited by Zachary Leader, McEwan remarks that fathers have sometimes been negatively presented in his work. Both his parents were aware of their relatively lowly class origins and truncated education, a source for McEwan's broad interest in the relationship between class, language, gender and identity, what he describes as the "layered linguistic density of English class", and more specifically in the power relations between men and women. At the age of eleven he was sent home from North Africa to attend Woolverstone Hall, a state boarding school in Suffolk, where the dislocating tendencies of a shift into the educated middle-classes placed McEwan in what he has called a "fruitful" state of linguistic and social exile. His fiction has regularly explored states of alienated tension with society and have sometimes been suffused with a sense of narrative detachment, even when dealing with the most horrific events, that gives them much of their disturbing power. As a fourteen-year-old teenager he read such novelists as Iris Murdoch and Graham Greene—an interesting literary apprenticeship given McEwan's characteristic fictional mix of an extended exploration of ideas with a journey into the darker areas of the human psyche.

Kafka was another early and significant influence that he has acknowledged in a number of interviews, most recently for the *Paris Review*: "My fascination with Kafka made me think that the most interesting fiction involved characters who could hang free of historical circumstance. But of course, nobody hangs free"(Begley, 2002). That tension between the desire for "hanging free" and socio-historical rootedness is key to much of his writing.

In 1967 McEwan went to Sussex University to read English, and on graduation in 1970 joined Malcolm Bradbury's pioneering Masters program in creative writing at the University of East Anglia. After completing his MA McEwan made what seemed at the time to be an obligatory student journey to Afghanistan and the North-West Frontier Province, later remembered for its ". . . long, long weeks of waiting. Boredom and smoking hash in huge quantities without any real point" (Hamilton, p. 17). The "hippy" culture that McEwan experimented with during this period re-emerges in a radically modified guise in the near-parody of an alternative community that appears in the later stages of *Enduring Love* when Joe visits the unstable and violent "family" of Steve, Daisy and Xan.

McEwan had begun writing fiction as an undergraduate and had sold his first story in 1972—"Homemade" appeared in *New American Review*—but it was in 1975 that he published his first collection of stories, *First Love, Last Rites*. This startling debut won the Somerset Maugham Award the following year. It is perhaps revealing that the word "love" appears in this often shocking, controversial collection, as it does in the later novel that is the subject of this book. In McEwan's early fiction love and human relationships are seen through the distorting prism of obsession, psychological breakdown, brutal violence and sexual perversion. As his work has progressed this concern with love in all its guises has remained as central as in this first collection, but the sense of extravagant excess (sometimes of gothic proportions) that pervades his early work has faded, allowing the moral urgency that is at the heart of his work to emerge ever more strongly. For the susceptible reader, the relentlessly challenging subject matter of *First Love* and the next collection of stories *In Between the Sheets* (1978)—summarized in Jack Slay's study of McEwan as "incest, murder, cross-dressing and paedophilia" (p. 12)—was made all the more disturbing by the clarity and cool detachment of McEwan's narrative style, an aspect of his writing that has been sustained and developed throughout his subsequent work. Commenting on this in a recently-published interview with Jonathan Reynolds, McEwan has cited Conrad's famous dictum from the preface to *The Nigger of the Narcissus* (1897). "My task which I am trying to achieve is, by the power of the written word, to make you hear, to make you feel—it is, before all, to make you *see*. That—and no more, and it is everything." In McEwan's terms, to sanitize human violence is to sentimentalize it and avoid true recognition of its horror. This need to face the reality of the human potential for destruction emerged strongly in his pieces for *The Guardian*, written in the immediate aftermath of the September 11 terrorist attacks on America, as well as in an interview he gave for the American television network, PBS:

. . . we are capable of acts of extraordinary destruction. I think it's inherent. I think one of the great tasks of art is really to explore that . . . I personally think the novel, above all forms in literature, is able to investigate human nature and try and understand those two sides, all those many, many sides of human nature. But I'm a little suspicious of the way we want to throw up our hands and just say, "Well, it's evil" (*Frontline* interviews: 3).

His first novel, *The Cement Garden* (1978), in which children conceal the death of their parents by burying them around the house in order to avoid being taken into the "care" of society, replicates the darkly macabre hues of the stories but focuses particularly on what has become a central theme in McEwan's work—the world of childhood, its various meanings and its relation to the "real" world of adulthood. In *The Cement Garden* the children create a self-contained world for themselves, albeit one that is uneasily charged with incestuous sexual longing—innocence in McEwan is always a problematic concept. The children's autonomy is necessarily relinquished at the end as patriarchal law is re-established but the novel inaugurates a fundamental tension in his work between patriarchal power and the apparently powerless—often embodied in female characters and children.

At the beginning of a decade that was to have a profound impact on the political dimension of McEwan's work, the 1980s, he briefly diverged from writing fiction and moved into writing screenplays, published in a collection entitled *The Imitation Game* (1981). One of the plays, *Jack Flea's Birthday Celebration*, had been written earlier in 1976 and shares some of the queasy tonalities of McEwan's early work. The two other screenplays, *Solid Geometry* and *The Imitation Game*, place a sharp focus on the theme of power relations between men and women. Deconstructing masculinity and femininity has become a key strategy in McEwan's writing and *Solid Geometry* (also an adaptation of an earlier short story) depends on a clear binary opposition between the two main characters, Albert the "eerily cold" rationalist as the author describes him in the script (p. 58) and Maisie his wife, a sympathetic representation of affective femininity. He is a scientist, employing some experimental physics to make his wife literally vanish as he twists her into a distorted shape. This bizarre act of erasure proved too much for the BBC who terminated the production before completion. *The Imitation Game* historicizes a comparable process of female disempowerment and silencing, using the 1940 setting of Bletchley Park, the now famous but then secret home of the Enigma code-breaking project, to portray the ways in which patriarchal orthodoxy represses female challenges to its hegemony. The independent and rebellious central character, Cathy, becomes romantically involved with Turner, the leader of the project, but discovers her own crucial secret: that he is impotent. By the end of the play she has been incarcerated in a prison cell for knowing too much about the project—but the actual knowledge she has gained that threatens the status quo is of the false notion of gender difference and the unequal power structures on which it is based. The introduction to *The Imitation Game* contains an important statement of McEwan's espousal of feminist thinking:

Patriarchy corrupts our most intimate relationships with comic and tragic consequences, and as a system it can be described in microcosm through its smallest and most potent unit, the family (p. 16).

Feminist critics had often reacted adversely to McEwan's early fiction and this explicit engagement with gender politics seems to denote a significant movement in his work that has undoubtedly remained a key concern. But this engagement may be a more complex affair than merely adopting a feminist stance. In his monograph on the writer, Kiernan Ryan suggests that *The Imitation Game* deliberately places the viewer in an ambiguous position:

The empathetic portrayal of Cathy's heroic defiance harbours a darker fantasy in which the predatory eye of the camera stalks a lone female to her doom . . . Not the least intriguing feature of McEwan's writing is that it knows it has a sinister side and is not prepared to disguise the fact, even if its progressive credentials end up muddied in the process (1994: p. 31).

The voyeur, the stalker, fantasy and power are all entangled within McEwan's view of human relations and although his later work seems to draw on the more naturalistic approaches of *The Imitation Game*, the sinister and unspoken (perhaps unspeakable) retain a powerful charge in his writing.

The title of the novel that followed McEwan's excursion into writing for television, *The Comfort of Strangers* (1981), was among his most overtly ironic. McEwan's titles always carry a multiplicity of meanings and paradoxes: *The Comfort of Strangers* is among his most *uncomfortable* books for the reader. The triangular relationship that is at the heart of the narrative, between the predatory, violent yet seductive Robert and the young English couple Colin and Mary ends in a bloody denouement for the latter. The setting of Venice allows for a range of intertextual resonances from Thomas Mann's 1912 novella to Nicolas Roeg's film of the Du Maurier story *Don't Look Now* (1973). McEwan had himself traveled to the city three years earlier with Penny Allen, whom he was to marry in 1982. The setting adds to the story's sense of dark fatalism and inevitability: a chance meeting with the murderous Robert leads the young couple to be drawn inexorably into his world of domination and subjection, as he stalks and then entraps them. This is no simple story of masculine will to power, though, since McEwan implies that the couple are complicit in their own fate. (Levels of complicity are always key issues in his work.) As Robert's manipulations take hold so their own sexual fantasies and longings come to the surface and they unconsciously or consciously adopt their role as victims with a disturbing willingness. As ever, McEwan draws our sometimes unwilling attention to what one critic has called the "unspeakable, the repressed . . . the signifying absences in our discourse." In doing so he again undermines any easy or easeful solutions to questions of human obsession and power—the kind of apparently comforting closure offered in the first of the concluding appendices to *Enduring Love*, where scientific explanation offers a reassuringly detached and clinical explanation of irrationality and psychopathic behavior.

The Comfort of Strangers, which was short-listed for the Booker Prize in 1981, was the first of McEwan's fictional texts to be adapted for film, appearing in 1990 in a version directed by Paul Schrader and scripted by the author in conjunction with Harold Pinter, whose plays sometimes seem to inhabit the same subversive space as McEwan's writing. Film versions have also been made of *The Cement Garden* (1993), *The Innocent* (1993) and *First Love, Last Rites* (1998). In 1993, McEwan had an unsuccessful excursion into the world of Hollywood movies when he wrote the screenplay for *The Good Son* (directed by Joseph Ruben), a film about a sociopathic child starring Macaulay Culkin in a less than angelic role.

An important feature of McEwan's career has been his willingness to branch away from the fictional prose form into other modes of writing. In 1982, he took what might be seen as his most radical step away from fiction when he wrote the libretto for British composer Michael Berkeley's oratorio *Or Shall We Die*, which was first performed in February 1983. In the same year, Stephen Frears's film, *The Ploughman's Lunch*, was first released. McEwan's screenplay for the film, for which he won the *Evening Standard* Award, offered a trenchant and cautionary satire on the dangers of misusing and manipulating the past, as the journalists and media people who inhabit the film represent history and the events of the present day through the distorting lens of a bankrupt political ideology. McEwan later collected the two together in a volume entitled *A Move Abroad* (1989) for which he wrote an important preface. Both works grew from a number of related circumstances, both personal and political. McEwan had just married (his first son was born in 1983), and at the same time the global political situation seemed to be deteriorating with the intensification of the Cold War by right-wing regimes in America and Britain. At home, the Thatcher government was well into its agenda of change, fueled by an aggressively individualistic ideology that McEwan found both repulsive and fascinating. In the preface to *A Move Abroad*, an important and revealing statement of his view on the creative act as well as the functions and limitations of the novel form, McEwan discusses the problems the novelist faces when attempting to reconcile ". . . the pleasurable surprise in the moment of writing" with "hard ideas, social theories, axes to grind, persuasive intentions or the determination to right" (1989: p. ix). The disputed borderlines between ideas, personal experience and political engagement are very much the spaces that particularly later McEwan novels inhabit as his characters negotiate questions, uncertainties and dilemmas. The problems that face the contemporary novelist are lucidly and candidly explored in the preface, a key text for those wanting insight into McEwan's thinking at this time and since, where he makes detailed references to other writers who are clearly important to him, amongst them George Orwell, the Czech novelist Milan Kundera and Salman Rushdie. *Or Shall We Die* poses questions about the uses to which humanity puts science, explicitly addressing the threat of nuclear annihilation. Hope for the future of humankind is seen as emerging from a paradigmatic shift in "our understanding of our place in the natural world." McEwan sees this as essentially "a shift from a Newtonian to an Einsteinian world view, or, in more general terms, from a masculine to a feminine consciousness or emphasis in our civilisation" (1989: p. xx). This power relationship between the masculine and feminine is a constant factor in McEwan's work, emerging in different ways in different texts, and he has repeatedly acknowledged his sources in the writings of the women's movement as well as in the new physics.

As Kiernan Ryan suggests, the two works collected in *A Move Abroad* fed directly into McEwan's next novel, *A Child in Time* (1987), which won the author his first major prizes, the Whitbread Award and the Prix Femina. It looks forward to the mid-1990s and there are echoes of Orwell's dystopian vision of future society in the proto-authoritarian world of the text where the realities of 1980s life in Thatcherite Britain—increasing social exclusion, widening divisions between rich and poor and stridently conservative moral attitudes—are pushed even further. The novel in fact features a character of unspecified gender, the Prime Minister, whose authoritarian right-wing government has prepared a government report on childcare to impose its dictatorial notions of "family values." As in so many of McEwan's texts, the central figure is a successful writer, in this case an author of children's books. Incidentally, this is a genre to which McEwan has made two contributions of his own, a picture book, *Rose Blanche*, published in 1985 and *The Daydreamer* (1994), a series of surreal stories about a boy who dreams his way into other identities. The latter has illustrations by Anthony Browne, whose own work also explores the thin line between ordinary and extraordinary, dream and reality. At first glance it may seem surprising that the author of *First Love, Last Rites* should work in this genre, but children and childhood are always central to McEwan's vision of the world, always a reference point and touchstone.

As in the later *Enduring Love, The Child in Time* opens with a single defining event, the abduction and disappearance of the narrator Stephen Lewis's three-year-old daughter. The tremors that reverberate from this traumatic moment provide much of the novel's subject matter as the narrator emerges from his self-imposed internal exile and estrangement, both from his wife and society at large. He becomes involved in the writing of the government report on child care only to find that it has been written already by his friend Charles Darke, a high-flyer in the Conservative Party. In the course of the novel, Stephen reshapes his life and in the process gains a heightened awareness of himself and those closest to him. This process is catalyzed by a central moment in the novel where Stephen has a vision of his own past, in fact his parents' past, as they discuss whether to keep the unborn child (Stephen) that his as yet unmarried mother is carrying. Birth and rebirth are powerful images in the novel and carry major significance for the novel's two central male characters. Charles, the narrator's closest friend and political aspirant, has a breakdown, abandons his successful but corruptive political career and regresses back into a boyhood world of outdoor adventures that eventually destroys him, trapped as he is in a traditional and conventional construction of masculinity. The novel ends movingly, with an account of an actual birth, suggesting the emergence of a feminized world that contrasts with the dystopian vision of society depicted elsewhere in the novel—"womanly times," as they are described in *Or Shall We Die*—that offer the narrator a renewed selfhood.

Time, history, the past—the way we use or misuse the past on private and public levels—the circular rather than linear nature of time—the relationship between single, epiphanic moments of time and larger expanses—all these have emerged strongly out of McEwan's work in the 1980s to shape and inform his later writing from 1990 to the present time. Alongside this has been a continued willingness to experiment with form and narrative—to draw on and merge a wide range of fictional genres, from thriller to spy novel to historical novel to the novel of ideas. If McEwan's early work often trapped the reader in the darkly confined, sometimes fetid spaces of consciousness and fantasy, the later work opens up into a wider historical daylight whilst maintaining a nagging sense of inwardness, obsession, repression and denial. Three of McEwan's later works, *The Innocent* (1990), *Black Dogs* (1992) and *Atonement* (2001), seem linked by this probing of the past/present dynamic. *The Innocent* (1990) continues the exploration of Cold War politics by setting the action in Berlin in the mid-1950s at the high-tension moment between Americans and Russians (the British increasingly marginalized and unimportant in the new world order). Often overlooked is the novel's subtitle, *A Special Relationship*, which puns not only on the central love affair between the two main characters, the "innocent" Leonard and the "experienced" German woman Maria, but also on the US/UK axis which is turning rapidly toward America as it becomes the post-war superpower in military, political and cultural terms, and British global influence wanes into its twilight years. The novel is a powerful mix of "noirish" Berlin settings (Isherwood with a strong dash of Le Carré), historical retrospection (the postscript is set in 1987 and foretells the fall of the Berlin wall) and Kafkaesque nightmare. Kiernan Ryan suggests that the *mise-en-scène* of the spy novel offers an appropriate metaphor for McEwan's fictional art. "Tunnelling down beneath the surface and burrowing across borders into forbidden territory to hijack and crack coded messages is a perfect image for what McEwan's fiction is up to" (1994: p. 59). In *The Innocent* this world of secrets and codes is juxtaposed with an extended moment of quite horrific revelation when McEwan gives us a relentless close-up account of the dismemberment and disposal of a murdered body. As the innards of the dead body literally unravel before us in an unstoppable flood of gore, borders between internal and external break down and the body as a containing force seems to collapse and fall. At one level this suggests the vanity of human wishes when faced with the physical realities of corporeal death but there is much more to it than a *memento mori*. Politics and history, the games that nations play, also seem to collapse along with the body, though the postscript in the final chapter seems to offer the possibility of redemption for the central figures. It would make an intriguing thesis to consider the increasingly frequent use of such devices in recent fiction, a sign perhaps that the borders of the novel are always suffering slippage and loss of definition—see for example A.S. Byatt's *Possession* (1990) and Margaret Atwood's *The Hand-maid's Tale* (1996). McEwan, of course, returns to the appendix again in *Enduring Love*, where the reader is offered an apparently authentic scientific case study on De Clérambault's syndrome as well as a final letter from the obsessive Jed, now incarcerated in a psychiatric institution.

Black Dogs, which followed in 1992, partially repeats the setting of Berlin at the time of the collapse of the wall. In fact, McEwan locates the narrative quite precisely in a set of time frames, from England and Germany of the late 1980s going back to France in 1946, the period immediately after the end of World War II. The explicit focus on the history of Europe in the second half of the twentieth century allows him to explore the tension between idealism and reality as it emerges from the history and politics of the epoch. The novel has a characteristic trio of characters at its center—Jeremy, as often in McEwan's fiction a writer and publisher, narrates his memoir of Bernard and June, a politically-committed couple who act as surrogate parents for him and whose daughter he marries. In the preface that precedes the narrative, Jeremy reveals the ways in which Bernard and June embody a dichotomy between rationalism and faith that is fundamental to the dynamics of McEwan's writing:

Rationalist and mystic, commissar and yogi, joiner and abstainer, scientist and intuitionist, Bernard and June are the extremities, the twin poles along whose slippery axis my own unbelief slithers and never comes to rest (p. 19).

Although Jeremy is in no way a self-portrait, the intellectual and emotional struggle described above seems close to debates that characteristically drive a McEwan novel and which are at the heart of *Enduring Love*. McEwan here seems to offer a fairly conventionally-gendered account of masculine logic set against female instinct, but this is alleviated by the disturbing account of the incident that gives the novel its name. June's encounter with a pair of wild dogs in 1946 rural France takes on an almost mythic and certainly symbolic status as she interprets the event as a sign of the existence of a powerful evil force determining human history. These terrifying dogs of war, with which June has a deeply disturbing encounter, carry a portent and warning of the apparent power and inevitability of destructive forces within the world. It's another example of McEwan's desire to face up to such possibilities while exploring positive alternatives. In *The Child in Time* and *The Innocent*, he offers the possibility of change and rebirth. In *Black Dogs* we are left with a foreboding prediction that the eponymous black dogs "will return to haunt us, somewhere in Europe, in another time" (p. 174). The problem of seeing and knowing, the gaps between mind and perception, clearly fascinate McEwan, and his writing is populated by observer figures, often writers, who attempt to draw together some of these irresolvable tensions—it's as though McEwan dramatizes and fictionalizes in them some of the persistent questions that haunt him as a writer. The tangled web of epistemological doubt that McEwan returns to explore again and again is clearly signposted in one of the epigraphs that precedes the novel, where he quotes from the Renaissance philosopher Ficino: "In these times I don't, in a manner of speaking, know what I want; perhaps I don't want what I know and want what I don't know."

McEwan's writing is so often characterized by a projected sense of evil as he tries to imagine the worst thing possible in order to get hold of the good. This is well illustrated in *Black Dogs* where June's terrifying encounter radically alters her life: "I haven't mythologized those animals, I've made use of them. They set me free. I discovered something" (p. 59). This positive outcome may go some way to undermining the popular, if misguided, view of McEwan as a deeply and darkly pessimistic writer. It has also led to criticism of his work as lacking in real political engagement. His characters retreat when they can into the safer world of the private and personal in the face of a late-twentieth-century reality that is too bleak to face. McEwan's characters often have their belief systems tested to near destruction by events that overturn settled experience. Sometimes they don't survive the ordeal, and his unflinching gaze on the fallibility of humanity makes the endorsement of political solutions a difficult, if not impossible, option. The solipsistic world of first person narrative that is interestingly a favorite device of McEwan as well as contemporaries such as Graham Swift and Kazuo Ishiguro reinforces this sense of alienated consciousness.

The period before the publication of *Enduring Love* was a difficult one in McEwan's personal life. His marriage to his first wife, Penny Allen, ended in 1995. The break-up resulted in a distressingly public legal battle over the custody of their children, which McEwan eventually won. In an interview with Kate Kellaway entitled "At Home with his Worries" that appeared in *The Observer* (September 16, 2001) McEwan talks engagingly and candidly about this period in his life and about the importance of his children to him. He also describes his working methods "at home" in his house in North Oxford:

"Sometimes I accept that I will have to write in 25 minute bursts." It is a "discipline" he adds. Often, he gets up for his boys at the "unbohemian hour of 7.30" and knows that in a school day there is a limit to how much he can do. And yet he is able to find amazing stretches of uninterrupted time: "If I think I am on to something, I'll just keep going for 12 or 14 hours." It is a thrilling feeling, everything is accelerated, heightened. Like a love affair? "Yes," he says.

The publication of *Enduring Love* in 1997 was rapidly followed by *Amsterdam* in 1998 and *Atonement* in 2001. In 1999 he was awarded the Shakespeare Prize by the Alfred Toepfer Foundation, Hamburg and indeed this period might be seen as something of a climax in McEwan's writing career thus far. *Amsterdam* finally won him the prestigious Booker prize. *Atonement* was short-listed for the same prize and has proven to be a very considerable popular success, selling nearly half a million copies to date in paperback. In between the appearance of these two works he was awarded the CBE in 2000. *Amsterdam* was perhaps a surprising novel to win the Booker since in many ways it seems to inhabit the world of social satire — Evelyn

Waugh rather than Kafka seems to be the prevailing influence. The novel continues McEwan's dissection of post-Thatcherite English society that began with *A Child in Time*, but without that novel's sustained exploration of epistemological and ontological uncertainty. The novel characteristically begins with a single event, a funeral that draws together a group of people — in this case a triumvirate consisting of a newspaper editor, a classical composer and the Foreign Secretary of a Conservative government — who react upon each other and determine each other's fates. In the course of the novel, the duplicities and deceptions of contemporary politics and media are gradually laid bare for dissection and mockery. Perhaps the most interesting aspect of the novel is its concern with the nature of creativity itself. Writers are often featured as central figures in McEwan's novels, enabling an ongoing debate on the relationship between language and reality, words and experience, individual perception and commonality of experience. In *Amsterdam*, McEwan makes use of the composer figure, Clive Linley, to explore the processes of artistic creation. But like everything in *Amsterdam*, Linley is seen through the precise lens of a narrative that relentlessly exposes the individual's capacity for self-deception and hypocrisy. Linley intimates to himself, without irony, that he is ". . . a genius" while engaged in a struggle over the final moments of a commission which ends in his plagiarizing the final moments of Beethoven's *Ode to Joy*. The novel ends in a macabre and deathly endgame involving the composer Linley and his friend Vernon Halliday, a newspaper editor staking all on an exposé of the Tory politician, which takes place in the eponymous capital city.

If *Amsterdam* demonstrates McEwan's credentials as a social satirist of no mean stature, then *Atonement* represents his most sustained and serious interrogation of personal and public moralities, truths and ideals. If Evelyn Waugh seemed to stalk the pages of his previous novel, then *Atonement* is initially set in classic Waugh country, the

English country house between World Wars I and II. But the narrative soon moves away from a pastiche of 1930s social satire. The initial setting for the novel is a late-nineteenth-century Gothic mansion in Surrey, home of the wealthy Tallis family during a summer heat wave in 1935. The rural idyll, with its echoes of Englishness in the family name redolent of the Tudor composer, is highly deceptive, though, as conflict at familial and geopolitical levels is always in the background. Interestingly McEwan uses this setting to write with great subtlety on the nuances of the English class system. In the absence of parental figures (the father is away on mysterious business at the Ministry of Defense, the mother withdrawn and sickly), the central narrator figure, teenage daughter Briony, takes control. She epitomizes a kind of unyielding adolescent certainty and inflexibility; the child here is aggressor rather than victim, and is herself an aspirant writer. Not long into the narrative, Briony has accused an innocent protégé of the family, Robbie, of rape, potentially destroying his life as well as blighting her own. Her later "atonement" is in part the origin of the novel's title as well as the origin of the novel the reader discovers she is writing as we move forward in time to the late-twentieth-century at the end of the narrative. Writers and writing of the early-twentieth-century—Woolf, Orwell, Elizabeth Bowen, Rosamond Lehman—haunt the novel as well as its central figure. As McEwan has said, "it's a novel full of other writers" (Reynolds and Noakes, 2002: p. 19). It's almost as if McEwan himself is working his way back in time as a writer, from the modernist period to the nineteenth-century classic realist text. *Atonement* sometimes seems like a meditation on the tradition and function of the English novel and McEwan has spoken in interview of the "perfection" of the nineteenth-century novel: "I think, in the creation of character, the great nineteenth-century novels are unsurpassed, and I think that I might push forward in my own little projects to make my novels more character-led" (Reynolds and Noakes, 2002: p. 23). The note

of slight self-deprecation belies the fact that *Atonement* has been far
and away his most critically praised and popular novel, but does suggest McEwan's desire to continue the re-evaluation of what the
twenty-first-century writer owes to the canonical writers of the nine-
teenth century that A.S. Byatt initiated in *Possession* in 1990.

The epigraph for *Atonement* is a quotation from Jane Austen's
Northanger Abbey where the heroine, Catherine Morland is up-
braided by Henry Tilney for her over-active imagination which has
led to her believing that horrible deeds of Gothic proportions have
been committed at the Abbey by Tilney's father. McEwan's interest
here, as elsewhere in his fiction, is in storytelling—particularly the
telling of stories that fail to distinguish truth from illusion, appearance from reality. *Atonement* deals with the aftermath of the central
character's catastrophic misapprehension of the truth and her conse-
quent use of fiction to retrace memory in an act of reparation that
can't be fully achieved in reality. But the extraordinary scope of the
novel allows McEwan to set this private accusation and expiation
against the backdrop of World War II and global conflict. The two
are particularly interwoven in the central scenes of the novel where
the wrongly-accused Robbie is swept up in the chaotic English with-
drawal from Dunkirk. Robbie himself makes the connection that offers a damning indictment of English society "a dead civilization.
First his own life ruined, then everybody else's" (p. 217). However,
this is one of a number of judgments and the novel can be read as
suggesting that the legacy of history is not solely death and disillu-
sion. As Hermione Lee suggested in a review in *The Observer* (September 23, 2001) ". . . a great deal does survive at the end of the
novel: family, children, memory, writing, perhaps even love and forgiveness. Or perhaps not; it depends on which of the controlling
novelist's endings we decide to believe in, as we hold this fragile
shape of the unified fictional work in our mind's eye, and we are
made aware how easily it can all fall apart." It certainly seems that

McEwan's most recent novel has struck some kind of powerful resonance with the reading public and the extraordinary popular success of *Atonement*—it achieved third place in the UK list of best-selling books in 2002—has confirmed McEwan's place as perhaps the most significant British novelist of his generation.

2

The Novel

The Title

The title tells us to expect a story about love, and the idea of *enduring* love might well be taken to indicate that this will be a kind of ideal love, a love that lasts despite whatever tribulations it may be put through. This is, in a sense, fair enough—the novel is an account of the relationship between Joe Rose and Clarissa Mellon, a relationship that comes under the most intense pressure and eventually breaks down when intruded upon by a third party, Jed Parry, delusionally convinced that Joe is in love with him. Joe and Clarissa's love *does* ultimately endure, and despite parting they are in the end reconciled and adopt a child (p. 242). However, the novel plays with the idea of enduring love in two significant ways—first, in playing upon the ambiguity of the word "enduring": does this mean a love that endures or a love that is endured, in the sense of suffered? It is Joe's lot to endure the "pathological love" (p. 128) of Jed, an experience which drives him to breaking point. Second, the novel ends up suggesting that the most genuinely enduring (in the sense of "lasting") love might be that "pathological love" embodied by Jed. The title and its resonances throughout the story as the issue of love is explored provoke questions about the nature of love itself, about sanity and insanity, and about the line between love and obsession.

Enduring Love explores both senses of "enduring"; it is both the story of a love that endures and a love that is endured; it is both the story of a love that we recognize as normal and a love that is identified as pathological.

The ambiguity of "enduring" also suggests a further connection with one of the main themes of *Enduring Love*: reading. Faced with a word that has more than one meaning, how does a reader interpret it? It seems appropriate to relate the issue of ambiguity to the theme of reading since the main characters of the novel are themselves readers. Clarissa, Keats scholar and university teacher of literature, is the most obvious reader, while Joe spends his time in the reading room of the London Library doing research for the article he is writing (pp. 40–41).

How to read the novel

McEwan himself describes *Enduring Love* as a "novel of ideas" (The *Salon* Interview), and as this discussion will suggest, it engages with some large philosophical issues, such as ways in which we can (or can't) know and make sense of the world. One way to approach the novel, then, is to think of the characters as representing certain ideas which the novel is setting out to explore. Reading, in a rather broad sense, is one of these. Not only are we the literal readers of the text in which Joe, Clarissa, and the other characters have their existence, but all of us engage in reading in its widest sense—we "read" situations, experiences, even each other, all the time. And so do the characters in the novel.

Joe, Clarissa and Jed can each be seen as standing for particular ways of reading, particular ways of looking at the world and interpreting it. Joe can clearly be seen as the representative of a rational, scientific mind-set—McEwan has described him as "a man steeped in science, in rationalism" (Capitola Interview, 1998: p. 2), and as Harriet Meyer comments in an early review of *Enduring Love*, "science is not merely what he writes about but the lens of his world-view" (1998: p. 279), while Clarissa, as befits her occupation and interests, tends to see things through the lens of canonical high art and literature. When she witnesses the fall of John Logan from the balloon in the accident that begins the story, "a scrap of Milton . . . flashe[s] before her: *Hurl'd headlong flaming from th' Ethereal Sky*" (p. 29). Jed Parry, we learn, suffers from a particular form of mental illness, De Clérambault's syndrome, which also functions as "the lens of his world-view"—he interprets everything he sees as a sign that Joe loves him, finding messages to this effect in the movement of Joe's curtains or in the traces of his hand moving over a hedge (pp. 78, 96). In this sense it is not only Joe and Clarissa, but also Jed, who can be described as readers. Furthermore, Jed is also, in an idiosyncratic way, religious, and sees God in everything and everything in terms of God—this contrasts with Joe's secular, rational system of thought, and has led some critics to see the novel as centrally concerned with the conflict between religion and science.

So one way of reading the novel is to consider the ways in which the characters themselves "read" the world, situations, experiences and each other. The ambiguity of the title demonstrates that the same word may be interpreted in different, or even contradictory, ways—a love that endures is clearly a *positive* notion; a love that is endured is just as clearly a *negative* one. One of the things that *Enduring Love* does is to set up a range of different methods of interpretation, ways of reading, which are at odds with each other: the idea of contradiction is worked out through the course of the narrative and in the interactions between the characters.

The Postmodern

Any novel is of course a product of its time. *Enduring Love* demonstrates an engagement with some of the issues and ideas that have in recent years been identified with the concept of the postmodern. Although this concept is a complicated one, and it has been said that there are as many different definitions of the postmodern as there are thinkers, it is a particular postmodern perspective on narrative that may be useful in reading *Enduring Love*.

Jean-François Lyotard has defined the postmodern as "incredulity towards metanarratives" (1984: p. xxiv); the meta- , master or grand narratives he was referring to are those accounts of the world (or the universe, or some part of it) which have claimed to be more than stories, to be true (this is one way of understanding the prefix "meta- "). These would include, say, history, and, more significantly for *Enduring Love*, science. These grand narratives told stories of human progress, and one specific reason for incredulity toward them is the evidence offered by the twentieth century that human beings have not progressed. For Lyotard, it is the Holocaust and Auschwitz in particular that call into doubt any claim that humanity has progressed.

According to this argument, incredulity is the result of the realization that those "metanarratives" were never anything more or other than narratives, that they are (just) stories, despite their claims to truth, objectivity and the like. Scientific accounts are themselves narratives, just as historical accounts are. This situation produces a paradox—suspicion of the narrative form gives rise to a sense that we should avoid narrating at all costs, yet at the same time there is the idea that there may be no other way for human beings to communicate, which suggests that we cannot *not* narrate.

One possible solution is found in what is termed the self-conscious or self-reflexive narrative—a kind of story which in various

ways reminds us that it is (just) a story. It is in this sense that *Enduring Love* can be considered to engage with the postmodern—it is
full of references to stories and storytelling, and also of reminders
that it is itself a story.

Beginning the Story

Enduring Love starts with the confident statement (characteristic, as
we see, of Joe): "the beginning is simple to mark" (p. 1). As Joe prepares to open a bottle of wine for the picnic he is having with Clarissa, they hear a man shout, and the next minute Joe is running
toward a hot-air balloon. There is a ten-year-old boy in the basket,
and a man trying to hold the balloon down by its ropes against the
violent gusting of the wind. Running toward it from different corners
of the field is a group of five men who have never met each other
before in their lives—together, they attempt to hold the balloon
down. As the wind grows stronger, it lifts the balloon and the men
find themselves leaving the ground. One by one, they let go of the
ropes. The balloon sails upward, with just one man, John Logan,
still hanging on to the rope. Eventually, he falls to his death.

McEwan has said of this incident that he "was looking for a device to bring together complete strangers, and to bring them together
in a kind of emotional heat" (The *Salon* Interview, 1999: p. 3). Two
of these complete strangers are Joe himself and Jed, whose chance
collision sets off the chain of events with which the rest of the novel
will be concerned. But to contradict the confidence of that opening
statement, in the second chapter Joe informs us that "[a] beginning
is an artifice" (p. 17), and lists a number of other moments he could
have selected as the starting-point for this story, such as the moment
when the picnic was planned, or when the route was planned.
"What recommends one [beginning] over another is how much

sense it makes of what follows" (pp. 17–18). The direct connection of a beginning with the theme of making sense is significant. This is also one of the ways of drawing readers' attention to the fact that they are reading a story, and indicates the self-consciousness or self-reflexivity of the narrative: "What idiocy," Joe reflects, "to be racing into this story and its labyrinths" (p. 1).

Somewhat later in the course of events, Joe returns to the question of beginnings, to suggest that he might have begun with the point at which he realized that Jed's pursuit of him was serious and disturbing (p. 73). The point is that a story must have a beginning—and in that sense the beginning *is* simple to mark—but that the choice of where to begin is arbitrary and is in the hands of the storyteller. *Enduring Love* will go on to develop notions of the arbitrary, the random, and their relationship to the telling of stories.

MAIN THEMES

Love and Selfishness

In the early stages of the narrative, Joe describes his relationship with Clarissa in terms that seem idyllic. He recalls the love letters she had written to him at the beginning of their relationship as "passionately abstract in their exploration of the ways in which our love was different from and superior to any that had ever existed" (p. 7). He admits somewhat ruefully that he himself had been unable to "match" those letters—"all that sincerity would permit me were the facts" (p. 7)—yet those facts seem miraculous enough to him: "a beautiful woman loved and wanting to be loved by a large, clumsy balding fellow who could hardly believe his luck" (p. 7). Immediately afterward, with his usual confidence, Joe states that he and Clarissa are "seven years into a childless marriage of love" (p. 8), at least implying that they are content with the situation. This is itself contradicted by his revelation of Clarissa's inability to have children herself, and of the "disabling grief" she showed at the death of a friend's four-week-old baby (p. 31). Further still, when the couple are finally reconciled, they adopt a child (p. 242). Perhaps this suggests that Joe's idea of love is not only at odds with Clarissa's, but is in itself limited. One of the devices McEwan has chosen to employ in *Enduring Love* is that of the first-person narrator, and one aspect of the first-person narrator is that she or he can only present a single and limited perspective on things—Joe can only tell the story from his own point of view. Clarissa's final letter gives quite a different perspective on events, implying another version of the story, and perhaps a rather different view of love. Jed's various love letters to Joe in turn give yet another angle, again different.

Jed's perspective on love is both delusional and obsessional. From the moment of his first chance encounter with Joe, he is certain that Joe is in love with him. He telephones, writes letters, and eventually, out of resentment and rage at Joe's failure to return his love, hires someone to kill Joe. Finally, he takes Clarissa prisoner at knife-point in her home and threatens to commit suicide if Joe will not assure him of forgiveness. Of course, like Joe, the reader can say that Jed is mad—his condition is such that it will in the end result in him being "held indefinitely at a secure mental hospital" (p. 238). Even here, he "writes daily" to Joe, and the novel ends with an example of one of his letters, still proclaiming his love and his conviction that it is reciprocated three years into his confinement (pp. 244–45). The psychiatric authorities conclude rather wryly that De Clérambault's syndrome "is indeed a most lasting form of love, often terminated only by the death of the patient" (p. 242), and in this way we return to the question of what "enduring love" might actually be.

However, in consideration of what love is, Joe himself thinks at one point that Jed's "pathological love" is a state which "must surely reveal . . . the nature of love itself":

De Clérambault's syndrome was a dark, distorting mirror that reflected and parodied a brighter world of lovers whose reckless abandon to their cause was sane (p. 128).

Dark and distorting, maybe, but a mirror nevertheless. Perhaps what Jed is doing is no more than what people in love ordinarily do. Lovers may well abandon themselves recklessly to their cause, while one individual in love with another may well seem fixated or even obsessed. Jed believes in love at first sight, as many people do; he believes that love conquers all; he believes that his and Joe's love is meant to be. In her review, Cressida Connolly suggested that:

What makes McEwan's depiction of the illness so compelling—and so alarming—is how close it seems to ordinary romantic attachment. The letters that Jed writes to Joe are like real love letters; his entreaties would be familiar to anyone who has suffered from unrequited love (1997: p. 3).

Perhaps love *is* a kind of madness, as Shakespeare suggested in *A Midsummer Night's Dream*:

> Lovers and madmen have such seething brains,
> Such shaping fantasies, that apprehend
> More than cool reason ever comprehends.
> The lunatic, the lover and the poet
> Are in imagination all compact:
> One sees more devils than vast hell can hold;
> That is the madman: the lover, all as frantic,
> Sees Helen's beauty in a brow of Egypt. . . . (V, i, 4–11)

To come a little more up to date, sex researcher John Money has suggested that when falling in love, "the person projects on to the partner an idealized and highly idiosyncratic image that diverges from the image of the partner as perceived by other people" (1981:

p. 65). Both Shakespeare and Money suggest that the beloved is no
more than an imaginary construction—just as Joe becomes Jed's
imaginary construction, merely a character in what Joe refers to as
his "private narrative" (p. 144).

Whatever their differences, and their different perspectives, Joe
and Clarissa's love has been mutual and reciprocal, intense, sustaining and affectionate. In her final letter to Joe, Clarissa herself describes it as happy, passionate and loyal (p. 219). Perhaps this
summarizes the qualities that love should have. One dictionary
definition of love is "that disposition or feeling with regard to a person which . . . manifests itself in solicitude for the welfare of the
[love] object, and usually also in delight in his [or her] presence and
desire for his [or her] approval" (*Oxford English Dictionary*). Love
consists in caring for the other person and in delight. It is clear that
Jed's is a warped version of such a relationship—self-absorbed, solipsistic, in the extreme.

And it is selfishness which *Enduring Love* contrasts and polarizes
with love, because selfishness means *not* caring for others. To return
to the beginning of the narrative, McEwan has stated that in relation
to the balloon accident, "the issue is selfishness." What appealed to
him about the apparently true story on which the incident is based
was "the dilemma of knowing that if you all hang on, you can bring
this balloon down to earth. But as soon as anyone breaks ranks, then
madness follows" (The *Salon* Interview 1999: p. 3). "If one [person]
lets go, it's crazy for anyone else to hang on" (*Capitola* Interview,
1998: p. 2). Of course, one person does let go, and Joe is very trou-
bled by the thought that the first to break ranks might have been
himself. In the end, we never discover who was the first to let go—a
gap in the story that implies that any story may be incomplete and
partial. But it could have been any of them, because, as Joe comments, "[s]elfishness is also written on our hearts" (p. 14).

Joe comes to recognize that this is part of Jed's problem, and that even his religious beliefs are bound up in his own self-centered universe. "God," in Jed's letters, Joe realizes, is no more than "a term interchangeable with self" (p. 152).

As Jed continues his relentless pursuit of Joe, Joe is increasingly driven into the kind of lonely isolation that mirrors that of his pursuer. He chooses not to tell Clarissa about Jed's first telephone call, something he describes as "my first serious mistake" (p. 37), erases the thirty-three answer-phone messages without showing them to Clarissa (p. 83), and comes to the conclusion that he is on his own, both in dealing with Jed and in trying to repair the breach with Clarissa that has taken place (pp. 149, 161). Clarissa's eventual analysis of what has happened focuses upon Joe's isolation, but suggests that in some way he brought the situation upon himself:

As the Parry thing grew I watched you go deeper into yourself and further and further away from me. You were manic, and driven, and very lonely. You were on a case, a mission. . . . [I]n the process you forgot to take me along with you (p. 217).

Joe's obsession with Jed is significantly described here as a process of forgetting to care for the other person, precisely what the *OED* definition of love suggests is crucial and even primary. The problem evoked by the novel's representation of love and selfishness is that while different individuals may see the world differently, they need to connect with others in caring relationships, because, as the poet John Donne put it in 1624, "no man is an island." Or, as Clarissa would know very well, Milton wrote that while God may be self-sufficient "not so is man," who "requires/Collateral love, and dearest amitie" (*Paradise Lost*, VIII, 425–6).

Reading

The incursion of Jed Parry, then, disrupts the relationship between Joe and Clarissa represented by Joe as previously ideal. Both Joe and Clarissa refer on different occasions to the "invasion" that Jed represents (pp. 103, 218). But from the very start, the two of them read the situation in entirely different and contradictory ways. Joe reacts with fear and suspicion (p. 53) and with hostility (p. 59). By contrast, when he tells Clarissa about Jed, she is in no way inclined to take the matter seriously:

> Some poor fellow has a crush on you and is trailing you about. Come on, it's a joke, Joe! It's a funny story you'll be telling your friends. At worst, it's a nuisance. You mustn't let it get to you (p. 58).

What we see from the two characters' reactions to the situation is primarily their differing interpretations of the same situation. Even though Joe says that at this point he "liked what [Clarissa] was saying" (p. 58), he *does* let Jed get to him in various ways. Most seriously, he allows Jed to drive a wedge between himself and Clarissa, telling her that "she was quite wrong" in her reading of the situation and in her dismissal of Jed as no more than "a nuisance" (p. 80). The division, the split between the two of them represented as a difference in readings, grows—it is worth noting that Clarissa refers to it here as "a funny *story*," and later as "the harassment *tale*" (p. 81), because this repeats the theme of the telling and making of stories. She herself, at least according to Joe's reconstruction of what she is thinking and feeling at this point, sees this difference as symptomatic—the two of them "happen to be in very different mental universes right now" (p. 82). She even begins to wonder whether Jed is a figment of Joe's imagination (p. 84).

Reading and readings are further referred to when Joe shows Jed's letter to Clarissa. She observes that "his writing's rather like yours"

(p. 100), clearly indicating that her suspicion that Joe might have invented Jed has not been allayed by the sight of Joe's evidence. This suspicion is a mark of the distrust that further divides and distances Joe and Clarissa from one another. Joe now begins to distrust Clarissa, wondering whether her insistence on reading the situation as she does is no more than a "front" (p. 108) to disguise the fact that she might be involved with someone else. In a crucial act of betrayal, he goes through her desk in an attempt to find some evidence of such an involvement, and although he finds nothing, the shame that this makes him feel becomes a further division between them because "now [he] really [does] have something to conceal from her" (p. 106).

This invasion of Clarissa's private space precisely mirrors the invasion of their lives by Jed. Clarissa significantly describes the ransacking of her desk in terms, once again, of reading, of signals and messages:

You even left the drawer open so I'd know when I came in. It's a statement, a message from you to me, it's a signal. The trouble is, I don't know what it means. . . . So spell it out for me now, Joe (p. 132).

As Jed's obsession with Joe—and, it must be said, Joe's obsession of a different kind with Jed—erodes the trust and love on which the relationship between Joe and Clarissa was founded, they reach the point where she like Jed, is trying to read, looking for signs, attempting to interpret. Meanwhile, Joe is doing the same, avidly researching De Clérambault's syndrome (p. 142), something which he has been impelled to do ever since he first managed to identify the syndrome, at which point Jed's love instantly became "a love whose morbidity I was now impatient to research" (p. 127). The tension between Joe and Clarissa comes to a head when she takes him to task for precisely this, angrily telling him, "You think you can read your way out of this" (p. 148). Immediately, though, she makes the division between them physical as well as psychological by moving into a separate room, something which becomes "a settled arrangement" (p. 149).

Now isolated from Clarissa, Joe continues to receive and read Jed's letters, which become increasingly threatening. His research into De Clérambault's syndrome has led him to anticipate that Jed will become violent, a belief that is borne out, despite the refusal of the police to take him any more seriously than Clarissa has, when Jed hires contract killers to shoot Joe in a restaurant. Though the wrong man gets shot, Jed eventually admits to Joe that "if you wouldn't return my love, I thought I'd rather have you dead" (p. 212), ironically adding "[i]t was insanity," as though the rest of his behavior were sane. Yet the shooting, which Joe sees as "confirmation of an absolute kind" of his own reading of the situation (p. 177), still fails to convince the police—his version of events at the restaurant do not tally in all particulars with those of other witnesses. The police conclude that, "Parry isn't behind this" (p. 182). Once again, this is an example of readings or interpretations which contradict one another.

Joe's world has been thoroughly disrupted and distorted. Jed's violence drives Joe to violence, as, having signally failed so far to "read [his] way out of this" by any of the acts of reading he has engaged in so far, Joe is reduced to leafing through an old address book, which turns up the name of a one-time criminal acquaintance through whom Joe resolves to get himself a gun. The acquisition of the gun allows him to defeat Jed, whose invasion has been completed by intruding into Joe and Clarissa's home and holding her at knifepoint. Pleading for Joe's forgiveness, Jed holds the knife to his own throat, at which point Joe shoots him in the elbow. But Joe has misread this situation: Clarissa is only further alienated from him, and leaves him, writing a letter that sums up the effects of their contradictory and conflicting readings of the events they have jointly and increasingly separately experienced:

A stranger invaded our lives, and the first thing that happened was that you became a stranger to me (p. 218).

Her letter concludes with a reflection on just how enduring their love may or may not have been:

I always thought our love was the kind that was meant to go on and on. Perhaps it will. I just don't know (p. 219).

In a sense, the novel here brings us back once again to its title, leaving readers, like Clarissa uncertain about whether this love will endure. Were the novel to end here, it would of course leave matters unresolved. The fact that it continues raises the issue of a theme that is closely related to the theme of reading, that of narrative and narration, of storytelling.

Stories and Storytelling

Stories emphasize cause and effect, the common-sense mode of understanding the world; stories give explanations. As *Enduring Love* is a kind of detective story, it can be useful to think of the detective story as a kind of model for stories in general. Beginning with a mystery, the detective story proceeds towards the solution of that mystery—if we can't work out for ourselves whodunnit (and why), we know that eventually the detective will assemble the suspects and tell them (and the reader) who did it, identifying the cause of the crime. But while common sense tells us that the effect comes after the cause, the particular shape of the detective story suggests that we experience the effect first and the cause later. So if stories support the common sense, cause and effect, view, experience in some ways contradicts it. The difference might be that while as Joe puts it, stories have "shape" (p. 36), experience is without shape. Conventionally, like the detective story, narratives advance toward a point at which all loose ends are tied up, problems solved, issues resolved (the marriage or marriages with which a Jane Austen novel or a Shakespearean comedy concludes can be similarly described). The technical term for this point of resolution is "closure," and this has been increasingly seen by contemporary thinkers and writers as problematic, partly because it goes against lived experience in which all too often loose ends remain and matters are not resolved. In short, closure is a fiction.

In *Enduring Love*, the characters try to interpret what happens by engaging in a variety of acts of reading. These acts of reading are the preliminary to acts of storytelling, as the characters also endeavor to make sense of things by making them into stories, shaping and ordering events and experiences into narratives. It is significant that the novel begins with an accident, because the balloon accident and the resulting death of John Logan have the immediate effect of disrupting both Joe and Clarissa's worldviews as they struggle to make some sense of what both, separately, suspect may be senseless (pp. 80, 83).

An accident, by its nature, is a random event. McEwan appears to have chosen the hot-air balloon (rather than, say, a car accident, which he has said he also considered) precisely to underline this element of the random. Joe observes that a balloon is a particularly "precarious form of transport when the wind, rather than the pilot, set[s] the course" (p. 5). That is to say, no human agency is in control; rather, balloonist and passenger are at the mercy of the wind, which can of course change direction, vary in strength, or drop entirely — it is outside, beyond, human control.

The death of Logan turns out to be particularly senseless since the ten-year-old boy in the balloon survives as it comes to rest by itself. The only loss of life is Logan's, who was attempting to save the child's life. "The impossible idea was that Logan had died for nothing," Joe remarks (p. 32). Clarissa says pleadingly, "it must mean something" (p. 32), and asks, "How do we begin to make sense of this?" (p. 33). Earlier, Jed has told Joe "we have to . . . make whatever sense of [this tragedy] we can" (p. 25). The accident in its randomness defies the sense-making impulse, and brings about a crisis in both Joe and Clarissa's worldviews exactly because it seems to make no sense. Staring at the dead Logan, Joe is struck by the thought that "[i]t was a random matter, who was alive or dead at any given time" (p. 19), while for Clarissa "Logan's fall was a challenge no angel could resist, and his death denied their existence" (p. 31). Randomness, chance and accident contradict the pattern and order which sense-making consists of.

The sense-making impulse expresses itself for both characters in the urge to tell stories. Joe and Clarissa tell each other the story of the balloon accident, something Joe describes as "hammering the unspeakable into forms of words, threading single perceptions into narrative" (p. 31). A little later, they tell each other stories of other events and experiences, as if to avoid confronting the disturbing matter of Logan's death, which is their real concern, and then, eventually, in the company of friends, telling that story again. Telling the story works both as a form of release and a kind of anaesthetic: Joe describes the way that:

our story was gaining in coherence; it had shape, and now it was spoken from a place of safety . . . it became possible to recount the events without re-living them in the faintest degree, without even remembering them (p. 36).

It is worth emphasizing the connection between the telling of stories and making sense. If an accident is something that defies the sense-making impulse, incorporating it into a story, which Joe significantly observes has "shape," somehow renders it bearable. Another way of putting this would be to suggest that the pattern and order (the "coherence") of story is itself a way of making sense.

A recurrent theme in much contemporary writing, both fiction and non-fiction, has been the suggestion that we make sense of experience in precisely this manner. The critic Linda Hutcheon, for instance, an influential writer on the postmodern, has used the term "narrativization" to describe the shaping of events and experiences into narrative, and proposes that "the process of narrativization has come to be seen as a central form of human comprehension, of imposition of meaning and formal coherence on the chaos of events" (1988: p. 121).

For Joe, science is the most significant and valid account of the world. He believes twentieth-century science to be "story-free." The day after the accident he seeks solace from its troubling implications by working on a piece about narrative in science. He is setting out to argue that nineteenth-century science can be distinguished from twentieth-century science by the former's reliance on story and anecdote; but as he writes, he becomes less and less confident about his own argument:

[M]y examples were fabulously skewed. . . . [W]hat in fact were the typical products of the twentieth-century scientific or pseudo-scientific mind? Anthropology, psychoanalysis—fabulation run riot. Using the highest methods of story-telling. . . . Freud had staked his claim on the veracity . . . of science. And what of those behaviourists and sociologists of the nineteen-twenties? It was as though an army of Balzacs had stormed the university departments and labs (p. 50).

Perhaps even science is a form of storytelling? Joe certainly implies that the neat separation of narrative from twentieth-century science doesn't work, and in this he and the novel are very much of their particular time: Christopher Norris, for example, has argued that "as the idea gains ground that *all* theory is a species of . . . narrative, so doubts emerge about the very possibility of *knowledge* as distinct from the various forms of narrative gratification" (1985: p. 23). In other words, can we express or communicate anything at all without making it into a story, or part of a story? Can there be knowledge that isn't narrative or—in Hutcheon's word—narrativized?

What is important is Joe's recognition that it is not just that "story-telling was deep in the nineteenth-century soul" (p. 48), but that it is a powerful human impulse, intimately connected with the desire to make sense, to make things made sense. It is possible to see science, or indeed any area of human knowledge as (no more than) another collection of stories. Joe's own preferred version is neo-Darwinism (p. 70), which offers an explanation of everything in terms of genetics, the great determinism of his—and our—time.

Clarissa, who, says Joe, "had generally taken against the whole project," describes neo-Darwinism as "rationalism gone berserk . . . the new fundamentalism" (p. 70), and an article on neo-Darwinism in the *Guardian* newspaper in 1998 provoked one reader to respond in similar vein:

[T]oday's ultra-Darwinists . . . [find] an evolutionary function for everything in modern society . . . But this is a game where it's impossible to lose. Earlier theorists who looked for divine functions never failed to find them either, even in the toughest cases. Wasps and nettles, for instance, existed to stir humans from their apathy, trivial insects to complete the natural order. And so forth.

The writer continued, "We are purpose-seeking animals. We long to find a meaning for everything, to build it into a tidy scheme and to project it on to the vast screen of our ignorance as a vision of the cosmos" (*Guardian*, February 8, 1998).

Though he asserts his own interest and affection for science, McEwan has himself expressed similar reservations about neo-Darwinism:

Everything, from love and commerce, to art and gratitude, has been explained—sometimes rather questionably—in evolutionary terms (*Guardian*, June 10, 1998).

Bearing in mind Harriet Meyer's comment, cited earlier, that "science is not merely what [Joe] writes about but the lens of his worldview," such reservations might be another indication of the partial and limited—even flawed—nature of that worldview. After all, Joe is not himself a scientist—as he is acutely aware—but a journalist, who is in the business of writing stories.

If *Enduring Love* suggests that stories are essentially ways in which we make sense of things, it then follows that "sense" is not something to be found in events or experiences themselves, but is something that we make—and make up. Like closure, perhaps sense and meaning are fictions with which we comfort ourselves in order to avoid facing up to the fact that reality may have no meaning. Jago Morrison has argued that the novel implies that storytelling is a "means of containment and control" (2001: p. 3), and the various narratives and kinds of narratives that the novel presents us with may then be seen as a range of strategies to contain and control the random flux of experience, what Linda Hutcheon terms "the chaos of events" (1988: p. 121).

The Problem of Knowledge

If the distinction between science and storytelling is eroded or called into question, as this discussion has argued, there are serious implications about the ways in which, and the extent to which, we can "know" the world. That McEwan is interested in such issues is indicated by the novel's insistent concern with science—*scientia* being the Latin for "knowledge." In the review cited earlier, Harriet Meyer comments that "science is so much the fabric of *Enduring Love* that the novel might be deemed another sort of 'science fiction'" (1998: p. 279). Insofar as *Enduring Love* is concerned with ways of knowing, it is concerned with what philosophers term epistemology, the theory of knowledge, which examines how human beings know about the world, what there is to be known, and how knowledge can be justified. It also considers the possibility that we can never know anything with certainty.

At the heart of *Enduring Love* we have Jed Parry and his absolute, unshakeable certainty that Joe is in love with him. Whatever Joe may say to the contrary, however vehemently he may contest Jed's interpretation of his words and actions, Jed "knows" he is right, as he repeatedly insists (pp. 63, 65, 67, for examples).

Joe is eventually able to identify Jed as suffering from De Clérambault's syndrome, a condition named after the French psychiatrist who treated a woman in the early part of the twentieth century who had become convinced that the King of England was in love with her:

This woman was convinced that all of London society was talking of her affair with the King, and that he was deeply perturbed. . . . The one thing she knew for certain was that the King loved her. She loved him in return, but she resented him bitterly. He turned her away, and yet he never stopped giving her hope. He sent her signals that she alone could read, and he let her know that however embarrassing and inappropriate, he loved her and always would. He used the curtains in the windows of Buckingham Palace to communicate with her. She lived her life in the prison gloom of this delusion (pp. 123–4).

It gives Joe great satisfaction to be able to diagnose Jed's condition because it offers him a kind of closure, a solution—he knows. He has pinned Jed down and is now able to attach a label to him, to define him and classify him. Once again, this is wholly in keeping with Joe's scientific worldview—one of the bases on which science proceeds is on the basis of classification and taxonomy. Once diagnosed to Joe's satisfaction, Jed becomes "a classic case" (p. 157) of De Clérambault's syndrome—that is, no longer a person, an individual, but a medico-scientific, psychological, "case."

The satisfaction Joe derives from being able to put a name to Jed's condition, however, goes further. First, it satisfies Joe's desire for rational explanation, and the desire for explanation has been identified as one of the sources of narrative satisfaction, a reason why people tell stories. But Joe says that a syndrome is "a framework of prediction" (p. 124); naming Jed's condition gives Joe a sense of what to expect; Jed will act out the part prescribed for him by the "story" of what happens in "a classic case" of De Clérambault's syndrome.

If science for Joe and literature for Clarissa represent ways of knowing the world and making sense of it, De Clérambault's syndrome is, as suggested earlier, a similar kind of lens for Jed. De Clérambault's syndrome is a way of reading—Joe sees this clearly:

[Jed] crouched in a cell of his own devising, teasing out meanings . . . always scrutinising the physical world, its random placements and chaotic noise and colours, for the correlatives of his current emotional state—and always finding satisfaction (p. 143).

Joe thinks of Jed's way of reading the world as his "private narrative," wondering whether "the story require[s] no consistency at all" (p. 144). Once more the connection between reading, interpreting, and story is established.

Of course, to suggest that all knowledge may be storytelling is not to suggest that all ways of knowing are equal, or that all stories are as good as each other. While McEwan is clearly showing that there are limitations in Joe's scientific worldview—he has said that "there is something about Clarissa's take on the world that Joe badly needs" (The *Salon* Interview)—it is equally clear that the novel does not validate Jed's "take on the world." If De Clérambault's syndrome is a mirror, we must remember that it is a dark and distorting one.

Jean Logan

In a number of important senses, the issues raised by the above discussion can be seen clearly in the case of the minor character of Jean Logan.

Like the main characters, she too is trying to make sense of the tragic death of her husband in the balloon accident. Just like them, too, she does so by interpreting signs—reading—in order to construct a narrative. After the police return her husband's car to her, she finds the remains of a picnic and another woman's scarf in Logan's car and concludes that her husband was having an affair and that his death was caused by him "showing off to a girl" (p. 123); otherwise, she says, "this story doesn't make sense" (p. 122). Joe comments that this is "a narrative that only grief, the dementia of pain, could devise" (p. 123). Like many of the interpretations examined so far, Jean Logan's reading of the situation, and the narrative she constructs in the extremity of her grief, ultimately proves to be a misreading.

Joe unearths the truth—which may be a further indication that his approach, though flawed, may not be without value and validity. It turns out that Logan, on his way to a medical conference in London, had given a lift to an Oxford professor and the young female student with whom the professor was having an affair. The picnic belonged to these two and the scarf to the student. Because of the illicit nature of the affair, the professor and the student deliberately refrained from coming forward as witnesses. Hearing *this* story, Jean Logan can recognize her story as wrong. It might well be that McEwan makes the Oxford don a professor of logic in order once again to suggest that some narratives have more credibility than others—this, after all, is the true story.

In terms of its engagement with epistemological issues, then, *Enduring Love* sets up a number of competing ways of making sense, many of which contradict one another, as in the case of Jean Logan outlined here, in order to suggest that it may in the end be the case that the desire for things to make sense is articulated through acts of reading and then through acts of storytelling; however, this does not mean that truth is forever unavailable, rather that more and less accurate versions of events are always in the process of being constructed.

If the novel finally discredits entirely Jed's method of reading and interpreting the world and indicates some of the flaws in Joe's method, perhaps it is Clarissa whose perspective is to be endorsed? After all, McEwan is in the business of literature, just as she is, and it has been argued that literature may go some way toward mitigating the problem of selfishness identified as one of the concerns of McEwan's novel: the contemporary philosopher Richard Rorty, for example, has proposed that literature is of particular value in teaching us to care about others—when reading a novel, we care about the characters and about what happens to them (Rorty, 1989: p. 14).

McEwan has commented that "Joe has a lack of emotional awareness" (*Capitola* Interview, 1998: p. 3) and his suggestion that there is something in Clarissa's view of things that Joe needs has already been noted—both comments would suggest an endorsement of Clarissa's sensitive, caring worldview.

Gender and Sexuality

In broadly linking Clarissa with emotion and Joe with reason, McEwan may be accused of simply endorsing gender stereotypes. The connection of femininity with emotion and masculinity with rationality is traditional and conventional, and has historically been used to women's disadvantage to argue that the possession of emotion is at the expense of reason. Therefore, in their emotionalism, women are irrational. Such a reading of *Enduring Love* is possible—it is true that Clarissa is beautiful, sensitive and imaginative, sympathetic and connected through her interest in the poetry of John Keats to a Romantic sensibility—but McEwan is arguably doing something more complicated—and more interesting—than merely underlining stereotypes.

Although Joe can be seen as stereotypically masculine in some ways—in his desire to master Jed through knowledge; in his dominance of the narrative (only in their letters do Jed and Clarissa get to speak for themselves, in their own voices); in his attempts to take charge of the situation—it seems to be going a bit far to describe him, as Jago Morrison does, in an article which will be discussed in Section 3, as representing "a moneyed, successful masculinity" (Morrison, 2001: p. 254), not least because of Joe's pervasive sense of himself as a failure, even a "parasite" (pp. 75, 99), because he is a journalist rather than a scientist. Having completed a draft of his article on narrative in nineteenth-century science, Joe reflects with some disgust that what he has written:

wasn't true. It wasn't written in pursuit of truth, it wasn't science. It was journalism, magazine journalism, whose ultimate standard was readability (p. 50).

Despite this sense of himself as a failure, it does seem reasonable enough to say that Joe's is a rather complacent masculinity which is very deeply threatened by Jed.

It is with intense discomfort that Joe finds himself out in the street talking to Jed about love, sex and getting to know each other, "terms more appropriate to an affair" (p. 67), and he describes the rupture that Jed has caused in Joe's very existence, which of course includes his gender:

It was as if I had fallen through a crack in my own existence, down into another life, another set of sexual preferences, another past history and future (p. 67).

What is particularly appalling to Joe is the idea that he has been sucked into "a *relationship*" (p. 73, McEwan's emphasis) with Jed, and it is of course a same-sex relationship. It does not seem an exaggeration to say, as Morrison does, that what this sets off in Joe is "a scrabbling for security" (Morrison, 2001: p. 254). Joe's immediate reaction is to try to invoke the law, something which he attempts to do on three separate occasions, in the effort to have Jed contained and dealt with and to protect his own threatened masculinity. Represented by the male authority figures of Duty Inspector Linley (p. 154) and Detective Constable Wallace (p. 182), the law that Joe is trying to call upon is itself clearly a masculine one. On each occasion, however, the law fails him, and indeed on the second, he is asked whether he is homosexual (p. 155)—it is as if the *"relationship"* with Jed has called Joe's sexuality into doubt. In desperation he is driven to take matters into his own hands, and he sets out to arm himself with a gun, a crude symbol of male potency. As he prepares to enter the absurd criminal underworld inhabited by ex-hippies-turned-coke-dealers-turned-property-dealers, Joe thinks he is exchanging "the illuminated envelope of fear and meticulous daydreaming" for "a hard-edged world of consequences" (p. 188). If Jed's attentions have turned Joe into a passive victim, if not actually feminizing him then at least depriving him of masculine power, this sounds like an exchange of a feminine situation for a masculine situation. What Joe wants—and has wanted all along—is to master the situation.

But instead of the affirmation of masculinity that he seeks, Joe finds only bizarre ambiguities. As he drives with his old acquaintance Johnny B. Well toward his rendezvous with the ex-hippies, he discovers that he does not even speak the language of this "hard-edged world," which turns out to be a language of circumlocution in which he is instructed by Johnny not to say "bullets" but "rounds," not to mention the gun, but to refer to "the item, or the wherewithal, or the necessary" (p. 189). As Johnny dozes off, Joe contemplates his moustache, which ought surely to be a signifier of masculinity, but finds himself wondering. "Was it flinty manhood women tasted . . . or yesterday's vindaloo?" (p. 190). When he reaches his destination, the confusions multiply—he first encounters Steve, who sports "a shaved head and a small waxed moustache," again apparent signs of an aggressive, assertive masculinity, but Steve's moustache is "dyed with henna" (p. 192), and "waxed to prissy Prussian points" (p. 194). The other man present, Xan, is first seen mopping the floor (p. 194), a domestic activity conventionally associated with the female, but "his huge forearms were hairless and meaty" (p. 194). Just before Joe leaves with the gun he has come for, he witnesses a fight break out between the two men, and his last view of them is of "Steve's head in the trembling vice of Xan's forearm" (p. 202). So despite the ambiguities, this section of the novel does end with Joe immersed in what Morrison calls "the banal narrative of male violence" (Morrison, 2001: p. 256).

Earlier, Joe's desire for masculine self-assertion took the form of his search for the knowledge that would enable him mentally to master Jed, by first identifying and then enthusiastically researching De Clérambault's syndrome. But the possibility of actual physical violence has not been far from his thoughts—in their first encounter in the street that so disturbs Joe, he finds himself "calculating the physical danger [Jed] presented":

I was bigger, and I still worked out, but I've never hit anyone in my life and he was twenty years younger, with big jointed knuckles, and a desperate cause—whatever it was. I straightened my back to make myself taller (p. 65).

The fear that he might come off worst implies Joe's insecurity. Nevertheless, Clarissa finally characterizes the interaction between the two men as a fight, telling Joe in her letter that "[f]rom day one you saw him as an opponent and you set about defeating him" (p. 218).

Finally armed, his masculinity reinforced, so to speak, he prepares to deal with Jed, though he fails to win Clarissa back by doing so. If shooting Jed is meant to be a triumphant reassertion of the masculinity Jed has threatened, this reassertion is highly compromised: it does not restore the lost heterosexual idyll but instead provokes Clarissa's disgust, and her departure.

For Joe has had a "relationship" with Jed—Clarissa is absolutely right when, just before she moves into the other bedroom, she says to Joe, "You're always thinking about him" (p. 148). Further, if this relationship has compromised Joe's masculinity in the ways suggested, it has also done so by putting an end to the sex which initially both find so comforting: "[w]e slept in the same bed," Joe confesses, before Clarissa moves, "but we didn't embrace" (p. 140), "we had lost the trick of love" (p. 140). He must wait to regain Clarissa until the story is taken up or taken over by other male authority figures, the psychiatric authorities, who (perhaps) finally succeed in containing Jed. Even then, what is clear is the lack in what Joe has initially described as the "childless marriage of love"—he and Clarissa are "reconciled and later successfully adopt a child" (p. 242), perhaps an acknowledgement of Clarissa's perspective rather than Joe's?

The section of the novel dealing with Joe's acquisition of the gun has not found favor with all readers: it is deplored by Cressida Connolly as "Hitchcockian melodrama" and as "ridiculous" (Connolly, 1997: p. 2), for example. But while the inclusion of this violent melodrama in a "novel of ideas" may be incongruous, that is surely the point—Jed has wrenched Joe's world from its moorings and in what seems a parody of Joe's neo-Darwinist ideas about evolution, shows him regressing to an irrational, thoroughly incongruous, and entirely desperate attempt to recover his lost or threatened masculinity in the most crude and primitive way.

But to return to the ways in which McEwan is doing something more than simply underlining stereotypes about gender we need to recall his statement, repeated in interviews, that there is something about Clarissa's "take on the world" that is lacking and is necessary in Joe. The conventional association of women with emotion has amounted to a devaluing of both women and emotion in Western thought—it's there, as Clarissa will know only too well, in Milton, where there are clear hierarchies both of gender ("He for God only, she for God in him") and also of what Milton refers to as the "faculties"—reason is God's supreme gift to humanity (*Paradise Lost.* V, 102) to which all the other faculties, in particular "fancy," the imagination, are supposed to be subordinate. Clarissa is able to "understand" Jed as "a lonely inadequate man" (p. 81), and to suggest asking him in for a cup of tea (p. 84), exactly what Duty Inspector Linley proposes (p. 157), and what, in her final letter to Joe, Clarissa suggests might have saved the situation (p. 218). *Enduring Love* shows the importance and the value—the essential value—of those so-called "feminine," so-called inferior, priorities and ways of thinking, showing that reason alone is not enough—it needs imagination, emotion, empathy. The gun is no guarantor of anything at all; rather, it is an indication of what (masculine) reason or reasoning masculinity can't do—connect meaningfully and productively with other people. It is in McEwan's insistence on the importance of those values that Clarissa stands for, and that have been undervalued through their association with the female or the feminine that he is going beyond the mere reiteration of gender stereotypes.

Ending/s

Just as it has suggested that a beginning is an arbitrary point, chosen by a storyteller in order to contribute to the shaping of experience which storytelling amounts to, in the interests of making sense, so *Enduring Love* has a number of different endings, which suggests a similar arbitrariness about the point at which a story is concluded. Two of these are presented in the form of "appendices" (which might be understood to mean that they are somehow subsidiary to the rest of the novel, though if so, why include them?). This discussion has identified the lack of resolution, the absence of narrative closure, which would have been the result of ending the novel with Clarissa's letter to Joe (p. 219) and her uncertainty about whether the relationship would endure. One of the important points that Clarissa makes in this letter emphasizes Joe's concern to set aside any possibility that it might have been him who first let go of the rope, and was therefore responsible for Logan's death (p. 217). This adds a further dimension to the theme of storytelling—the person telling the story may have a vested interest in the particular shape that the story takes. In Joe's case what is in it for him is self-exoneration, a disclaiming of responsibility for Logan's death. He has revealed both his uncertainty about who let go first and his desire to disclaim responsibility earlier in the course of his narration (pp. 15, 55).

The letter is followed by the ending of Jean Logan's story, with the important idea of the "true story"; then the first of the appendices, presented as a different kind of narrative altogether, a psychiatric case study, purportedly "reprinted from the *British Review of Psychiatry*," authored by Drs. Wenn and Camia (pp. 223–43).

The founder of psychoanalysis, Sigmund Freud, famously wrote up his various patients, such as "Dora" and "Little Hans", in the form of case studies, narratives which have often been described as having more in common with literary narratives than with scientific accounts, but the question raised by Clarissa's letter about the vested interest of the storyteller in the story that is being told applies here, too. When Freud wrote his case studies, he was doing so to prove the validity of his theories. He was also striving to get psychoanalysis recognized as a *science*, and so the case study offers a further slant on issues that have been explored earlier in the novel. Wenn and Camia, one can surmise, likewise have an interest in the story they are telling—publication of the case study in a medical journal will enhance their reputations. Additionally, their case study, like Freud's, validates the theory: De Clérambault was right. Cynically, one might say, Wenn and Camia are pinning their psychiatric credentials to the coattails of De Clérambault.

The case study appears to offer readers precisely that narrative closure which would have been denied by ending with Clarissa's letter, or even with Jean Logan's revision of her story. Recognizing the characters by their initials (in the case study, Clarissa Mellon is "M," Jed Parry "P" and Joe Rose "R"), we discover that "R and M were reconciled and later successfully adopted a child" (p. 242), so there is a happy ending to their story. The case of Jed seems also to be closed, now that he is safely contained in a "secure mental hospital" (p. 238) and although he continues to write to Joe on a daily basis, the letters are not forwarded "to protect R from further distress" (p. 239). The case study seems precisely to resolve the problems and issues that the story of Jed's invasion of the lives of Joe and Clarissa has raised.

But there are at least two twists. The names "Wenn" and "Camia" are an anagram of "Ian McEwan," at which point readers may well start to wonder if the whole thing is a game, since the case

study is so clearly a spoof. Is De Clérambault's syndrome a real psychological disorder? And how many of the texts listed in the case
study's bibliography are real? Without giving the game of the anagram away, Harriet Meyer did "wonder . . . whether the psychiatric
literature included in the novel is actual" (1998: p. 279). De Clérambault's syndrome is apparently a genuine condition (Connolly,
1997: p. 2), but it is one that is uniquely suited to McEwan's purpose
since it so clearly represents a system of reading and interpretation.

One effect of the case study might be to remind us that it is not
just beginnings that are artifices, but *all* narratives; not just novels
but psychiatric case studies too. Not just the stories of journalists but
also neo-Darwinian explanations of the world and other scientific
accounts as well, are made by human beings, who have in all cases
worked to give that "shape" that Joe talks about to events and experiences. If lived experience is random (as is implied by the balloon
accident) and chaotic, then *any* shape we give to it is artificial, any
explanation is constructed.

So the case study might actually destabilize the narrative closures
it seems to offer — if McEwan's anagram makes readers suspect that
a joke is being played, the joke might be on readers themselves. To
take up the point proposed in the previous section, perhaps the spu-
riousness of the case study might even, as Morrison argues, under-
mine whatever reaffirmation of norms, masculine, feminine,
heterosexual, rationalist, scientific, it seems to offer. Even if this isn't
the effect of the first appendix, in its second twist the novel gives the
last word to Jed Parry, allowing him to demonstrate that while he
may be safely contained, his case is by no means closed. Three years
after his confinement, a thousand days in prison, as he himself puts
it, Jed remains utterly convinced of his delusion, still supremely
confident that Joe loves him, still proclaiming his faith in God and
his faith in Joe. He still believes he is receiving messages from Joe,
even though we know from the previous appendix that his letters are

not being forwarded. He is not cured of De Clérambault's syndrome, and this serves as a way of leaving the story open, leaving at least one matter unresolved. If Jed is contained in one sense, then, he is not contained in another. To what extent have the psychiatric authorities managed to master Jed?

So it can be suggested that *Enduring Love* has it both ways in its ending: there is both closure and openness, just as we have both the story of a love that endures and a love that is endured. McEwan has said that the "random element in life is a gift to a novelist to make a pattern of it, to make some sense of it, to contest its meaning or even ask whether there's any meaning to it at all" ("Interview," 1998: p. 1). It is clear then that ideas about making sense, such as those that have been outlined in the foregoing discussion, were conscious ones, and that the question of whether there is meaning was intended. But he has also said that *Enduring Love* was written "in a spirit of investigation," and that he was not "try[ing] to give a lot of answers to either how people should live or whether one could live a good life by scientific method" (The *Salon* Interview, 1999: p. 5).

3

The Novel's Reception

As is often the case with McEwan's recent fiction, initial critical reaction to *Enduring Love* offered a wide range of responses, from the ecstatic to the dismissive. The distinguished novelist Anita Brookner's review in *The Spectator* described it as "brilliant" but Jason Cowley in *Prospect* expressed disappointment that McEwan "has become a high class thriller writer." The novel was widely praised for the clarity and lucidity with which it portrays contrary states of mind and being—from Joe's scientific rationalist/positivist viewpoint to Jed's obsessive and faith-driven compulsion that turns into a violent erotomania. Anita Brookner found it ". . . almost a miracle that the novel holds up under the strain" of this wide-ranging subject matter. Conversely, the reviewer in *New Woman* wrote of "the paucity of the material." "McEwan hopes to stir the currents of pathology and unease as he's done in the past. But so slight is his story that it all has to be supported by a lengthy appendix and case history from the *British Review of Psychiatry*" (September, 1997).

Criticism of the novel's engagement with contemporary scientific thought came from two rather more substantial reviews, Cressida Connolly's in the *Literary Review* and Amanda Craig's in the *New*

Statesman. The latter complained that the novel lacked originality because: "from *Middlemarch* to *Brazzaville Beach* novelists have mined science for metaphor and, perhaps, intellectual respectability. The trouble is, most of us have now read the same books, and we are not overly excited by having rationalist arguments repeated at third-hand in a work of fiction" (1997: p. 43). Rather more favorably-inclined critics expressed much admiration for McEwan's tight prose style—always a significant feature of his writing. "Clarity is a great virtue in writing," McEwan has affirmed. "There are certain scenes that can only succeed if the visual elements are attended to first, all else (the emotional aura, the conflict, the love, etc.) then follows, or even grows out of the visual detail" (*Bold Type*, 1998: p. 3). Reviewing the novel in *The New York Review of Books*, Rosemary Dinnage described him as "the quietest and most lucid of stylists, with never a word wasted or fumbled," suggesting the appropriateness of coining the term "McEwanesque" to describe a style that combines economy and visual power with the disturbing presence of menace and subtextual darkness. This hints also at his debt to Kafka, a literary influence that McEwan has often acknowledged in interviews. It is interesting to note in passing the repeated use of the term "beautiful" to describe McEwan's stylistic realisation of the novel—e.g. "Beautifully executed" (*Wall Street Journal*), "[A] beautifully realized novel . . ." (*Boston Globe*)—and even those reviewers who had reservations about the novel's structure or content heaped praise on McEwan's "impeccably written" prose (*The New York Review of Books*).

McEwan has spoken widely of his stylistic aims as a novelist, particularly the priority he has given at certain moments to clarity:

I've always wanted prose that has about it a great clarity. Having a scientist narrate this novel I was able to indulge my own taste for precision in what's happening. I like a sort of lambent clarity in the opening pages which then can dissolve into mystery (*Capitola* Interview: p. 3).

This seems to underline one of McEwan's most powerful attributes as a novelist—the capacity to apply scalpel-like verbal analysis to what one reviewer called "the back corridors of the psyche and the heart" (*Miami Herald*) while sustaining a vivid and often poetic discourse throughout the text. Although this combination of the precise and the poetic is characteristic of much of his work, it is most appropriate to the thematic concerns of *Enduring Love* as the novel traces the conflict between faith and reason, love and science. It is, as David Malcolm stresses, "a novel not just about psychological states, but more specifically about that central psychological state: love. Love is, indeed, one of the novel's main focuses—largely pathological love or the pathology of love, but love nonetheless" (2002: p. 172). In a perceptive review for *The Times* (August 23, 1997), Michelle Roberts also points to this aspect of the novel and McEwan's work in general:

Under their dark, bristling, thrillerish surfaces lurk explorations of the way we love now: men and women mostly, but parents and children too. . . . A constant image recurring in his work is the man-woman couple so tightly tangled together and at the same time so confused about sexual difference that an act of violence by a third party is required to get all the protagonists to separate. . . .

One aspect of the novel that did receive virtually unanimous acclaim was the beginning. Many readers and commentators have responded to the gripping narrative power of the first chapters which seem to carry the reader along as inexorably as the central characters are impelled by the unfolding series of events over which they attempt to assert control but largely fail. Even the reviewer for GQ, who otherwise found the novel "an overwritten psychological thriller," managed to be enthusiastic about the "wonderful" opening. The arresting, riveting opening is another characteristic McEwan device and perhaps embodies another tribute to Kafka—one only has to think of the extraordinary opening to *Metamorphosis*, where Kafka has his ordinary narrator undergo an extraordinary physical change in the first few lines, to make the connection. McEwan himself has noted this interest in what Joe Rose calls "a pinprick on the time map" yet which can form a defining, life-changing moment—a moment that he gives in all its intensity and power and then traces the rippling, expanding consequences:

Moments of crisis or danger represent a means of exploring characters—the strengths and defects of personality—while at the same time offering a degree of narrative interest: it's a matter of having your cake and eating it (*BoldType*: p. 1).

In another online interview McEwan describes the early stages of the writing of the novel:

I came across a journal entry I wrote about six months before I began working on *Enduring Love*. My journal tends to be full of little exhortations, and it said, "write a first chapter that would be the equivalent of a highly addictive drug." I did want to have the reader hit the ground running . . . In fact one of the other chapters was originally the opening. It's a chapter where someone makes an attempt on the life of the narrator in a restaurant (*Capitola* Interview: p. 1).

(It is perhaps fortunate that McEwan changed his mind about the opening of the novel since the restaurant scene has been criticized by some for being one of the less convincing moments in the novel.) Valerie Sayers noted in a review in *Commonweal* that "this is as stunning and promising a novel opening as I have read" (1998: p. 25). In a brief but illuminating piece she praises the way McEwan achieves a fine balance between "dramatic scene and philosophical narrative, between exterior reality and interior struggle" (1998: p.

24). She goes on to express some disappointment in the novel's failure to depict a serious challenge to Joe's rationalism from religious faith, since Jed's religion is, she feels, a rather woolly affair and turns out to be the belief of an apparent madman. The novelist and writer Alain de Botton neatly expressed the compulsive nature of the novel's opening when he described *Enduring Love* as "A page turner, with a plot so engrossing that it seems reckless to pick the book up in the evening if you plan to get any sleep that night" (*Daily Mail* September 5, 1997). McEwan seems to have been delighted that some readers have devoured the book in one go, seeing the writer/reader relationship as strangely analogous to the subject matter of his novel:

I'm pleased when people tell me that they sat down and read *Enduring Love* in one sitting. In that respect, writers are like jealous lovers: "I just want you to think of me" (*Capitola* Interview: p. 1).

As Sven Birkets noted in a review in the *New York Times Book Review*, the classic novel might be seen to have a "rising action" that leads to a climactic moment followed by denouement and some form of resolution. *Enduring Love* of course follows an entirely different narrative arc, with the climax coming right at the beginning, followed by what Birkets calls the "falling" action of characters reacting to the fissures that have opened up in their personal landscapes. Rising and falling is a motif that McEwan establishes right from the start, and within the ballooning incident is inscribed a whole series of significances; from a reworking of the fall of mankind (pursued in Jed's aggressive desire to redeem and save Joe) to a version of the Icarus myth that ironizes mankind's arrogant belief in the power of science to overcome nature. The highly dramatic opening becomes a kind of narrative crucible in which, as Birkets says, "identities and fates would buckle into new shapes." The danger that the opening might seem to be setting into motion a kind of narrative theorem which will test out mechanically characters' reactions to a central event is raised by Adam Mars-Jones in his *Observer* review (September 7, 1997: p. 16). Mars-Jones suggests that "it speaks well for Ian McEwan's descriptive powers and the fluency of his invention that this opening scene doesn't smell like essence of quandary . . . although his choice of profession for Joe, a popularising science writer, makes his mouthpieces almost too adept at analysing its implications." Joe's facility with rational analysis, which often seems in the novel to be an end in itself, leads Mars-Jones to deduce what he sees as the novel's "painful point," "that knowing more about the factors that determine your behaviour is not the same thing as becoming either freer or wiser."

4

The Novel's Performance

Although *Enduring Love* has not matched the popular and critical acclaim of *Atonement*, it has nonetheless proved to be among McEwan's most successful novels. It was shortlisted for the 1999 International Dublin IMPAC prize, the 1997 Whitbread and narrowly missed the shortlist for the Booker Prize, an award that proved somewhat elusive for McEwan until *Amsterdam*. *Enduring Love* is currently being adapted for film by screenwriter Joe Penhall and director Roger Michell. Since the novel's first appearance, it has become a staple element in undergraduate modules on the contemporary British novel as well as book groups and reading circles. The critical debate that has developed beyond the first reviews has focused on three areas in particular: the success or otherwise of the novel's narrative structure, McEwan's use of fake textual material at the end of the novel and, a topic that was touched on earlier, the representation of gender. In order to give a sense of the ongoing discussion that the novel has generated, this section will explore these issues in further detail and will consider the two longer studies of the text that have appeared since its publication.

Narrative Structure and Genre

Despite the general critical sense that the opening of the novel is among McEwan's finest work, indeed one of the best in any contemporary British novel, critics and readers of the novel have disagreed over the structure of the novel as a whole. The sheer power of the opening could be seen as a disadvantage to the rest of the novel in that the rest is something of an anti-climax—a common response among readers. David Malcolm relates this to what he sees as a characteristic fragmentariness in McEwan's fiction: "As in some of McEwan's novels, certain episodes seem to stand out as complete in themselves and somehow separate from the novel's main story material" (2002: p. 161). Jason Cowley sees this as a flaw in the writing, describing McEwan's novels as "narratives of moments. a series of imaginative set pieces which seldom coagulate into a fully realised work." (1998: p. 42). This rather harsh judgement fails to take account of what might be seen as a basically realist element in McEwan's writing—the awareness that experience, however much we may want to shape it into a coherent narrative, resists the imposition of order or patterning. Hence, the structure of his novels reflects the fragmented and apparently arbitrary nature of life.

Apart from the (perhaps) obvious sense that it is hard for the rest of the novel to maintain the kind of narrative pitch and drive established at the start, some have questioned whether McEwan allows plot considerations to take over in the later stages. This is partly a response to the way in which *Enduring Love* merges and mixes genres ranging from the novel of ideas, through the love story, to the detective thriller. The latter has been viewed in some quarters as the weakest part of the narrative as the story fragments into a thriller, as Joe descends into a shady, almost comically stereotyped criminal underworld and the novel gives us contract shootings in classy restaurants, hostage scenarios, sceptical cops and so on—all of which appear to belong in the world of Colin Dexter's Inspector Morse rather than a McEwan novel, where criminality is more often filtered through the lens of the gothic/grotesque. After these episodes, the novel switches back to the hyper-rational mode with the additional case study and appendices that appear to have the imprint of academic authority. Mars-Jones sees this shifting of genres as ultimately a weakness in the book's structure:

It's disappointing that a book that begins so full-throatedly should end with stagy confrontation, then case history, references and appendices (1997: p. 16).

This is a view that is echoed elsewhere in the novel's reception. For example, Elizabeth Judd, writing in the respected online journal *Salon*, praises the novel's capacity to bridge genres: "it's a psychological thriller, a meditation on the narrative impulse, a novel of ideas" (1998: p. 2) but then criticizes McEwan for "chasing stray plot lines when he could have been teasing out the complexities of the relationships between Parry, Joe and Clarissa." Cressida Connolly, in the *Literary Review*, found the later stages of the novel, particularly Jed's descent into "Hitchcockian melodrama" far from convincing. This connects with her view that the novel is overloaded with incident. "The book burgeons with coincidence, events and ideas: it's like getting three novels for the price of one" (1997: p. 3). A much reiterated comment on the novel is that it is concerned with how we tell stories, how we give form to chaos and how our necessary, even obsessive desire to shape experience into narrative can sometimes lead to false assumptions and conclusions (for example, Jean Logan's false narrative about her husband's infidelity, Parry's "love story" of his relationship to Joe). As we have already suggested, McEwan is also concerned with the implications for human relationships of the capacity of people to read the same event in a multiplicity of different ways. In many ways *Enduring Love* is full of textual self-awareness—after all, two of the central characters are concerned with writing and literature—and therefore, it seems wholly appropriate that it should feature a wide variety of different kinds of storytelling. Perhaps only the individual reader can decide whether or not McEwan succeeds in sustaining our interest in this meditation on the unreliable nature of narrative and of human selfhood. Writing in *Commonweal* Valerie Sayers suggests that the rescue attempt with which the novel ends provides a narrative thread that loops the story back to its opening. But she also suggests that ultimately "the story floats away as quickly as the balloon which set Joe Rose's ordeal in motion, and the current carrying it is plot. The ideas trying to anchor that plot drop one by one to the ground. Some of its most disturbing suggestions . . . are never fully explored" (1998: p. 26).

Appendices, Deceptions and False Trails

Another controversial aspect of the novel that has generated much critical debate is McEwan's use of two final appendices, one purporting to be an article on De Clérambault's syndrome (using Parry as the subject) from the *British Review of Pyschiatry* and the other a letter written by Parry to Joe from the psychiatric institution in which he is incarcerated. The multiplying of endings has become a convention of the postmodern novel ever since John Fowles gave the reader a choice of closures in his 1969 novel *The French Lieutenant's Woman*. The extra-textual additions here serve to add another layer of discourse to the already-rich variety of styles and genres that the novel contains. Interestingly, the final appendix allows Jed Parry—now the outcast and punished "madman"—a position of narrative authority since his is the last voice we hear. The main controversy, however, has revolved around the pastiche of an academic journal that forms the first appendix which was taken in some quarters as a genuine piece of scientific research. In an amusing article in *The Guardian* (August 16, 1999) entitled "Fooled You," Oliver Burkeman traces the brief history of McEwan's fake, the key to which is, of course, contained in the surnames of the supposed two authors—Wenn and Camia (the anagram of Ian McEwan). Laura Miller covers much the same ground in a piece for the online magazine *Salon* (September 21, 1999) rather more boldly entitled, "Ian McEwan Fools British Shrinks" and subtitled, "The Novelist Puts One Over on a Few American Critics, Too." It seems McEwan managed to trick a number of critics as well as psychiatrists into accepting the first appendix as genuine. The reviewer in the *New York Times* (January 15, 1998), Christopher Lehmann-Haupt, criticized the novel for being too factually based. "Mr. McEwan has simply stuck too close to the facts and failed to allow his imagination to invent." Sven Birkerts in the *New York Times Book Review* seemed inclined to take the appendix at face value:

Unless the appendix is an elaborate fiction, like the foreword to *Lolita* by John Ray Jr. PhD. Then we finally have to assume that McEwan is quoting an actual case history and modelling the events of the novel closely upon it. It is an impressive transformation, the rearing up of a fictional world around summary notions from the realm of the actual (1998: p. 7).

McEwan extended the charade by submitting the appendix in the name of one of the authors to the *Psychiatric Bulletin*. It wasn't published, but received a favorable review by a consultant psychiatrist at the National Hospital for Neurology and Neurosurgery in London, which described the novel as being "based on a published case report." Other psychiatrists were less persuaded by the veracity of the article and in an article in the August 1999 issue of the *Bulletin*, McEwan came clean, suggesting that, "If the monograph had been published, it would have seemed that my novel was based on a genuine case, my characters would have acquired an extra sheen of plausibility and the division between the real and the invented would have become seamless." Clearly McEwan was delighted by the success of his ruse but, more seriously, this latter comment taps straight into the heart of one of the novel's major concerns—the blurred line between fiction and reality—and so the hoax that he has perpetrated seems less like an elaborate confidence trick and more like an embodiment of one of the text's key issues. We have already cited another review of note in a scientific journal that appeared in the *Journal of the American Medical Association*. Its author, Harriet Meyer, offers a brief but sensitive reading of the novel that emphasizes the novel's lyricism, despite its scientific content and reminds us that "science and humanism tangle on the page." This radically contrasts with Cressida Connolly's view that the novel is "weighed down by a surfeit of scientific information" (1997: p. 3), and she ended her review with a plea for a moratorium on novelists reading works of science. "An author's individuality is drowned in this sea of science. Much as I enjoyed *Enduring Love*, I missed Ian McEwan." Similar reactions can be found in Amanda Craig's *New Statesman* review where she expresses some impatience with McEwan's "fascination with the scientific and the supernatural." But comments such as this seem to miss the way in which *Enduring Love* explores rationality, science and logic in conflict with irrational belief, or "magical thinking" as McEwan has called it in an interview. In *Enduring Love*, he develops and brings to a climax themes that have permeated much of the rest of his fiction. McEwan is very much in evidence here.

Further Questions of Gender

Just as the science/belief debate provides an essential intellectual landscape for this among a number of his novels, so the issue of gender construction permeates this and other McEwan texts. We have already noted his concern with the representation of masculinity and femininity in his other novels, and in particular his espousal of feminism as a force for constructive and positive change within the world at large. The "womanly times" that are cited in the libretto for the oratorio *Or Shall We Die*, which as Jago Morrison suggests, are "characterised as an amalgamation of maternal empathy and . . . the postpositivistic Einsteinian legacy in science," (Morrison, 2001: p. 256) are pitted against a masculine drive toward destruction that McEwan sees as pervading Western culture and politics. *Enduring Love* clearly continues this debate, but some initial reviewers felt uneasy about the apparent marginalization of those characters associated with the "feminine" — notably Clarissa and the stalker Jed Parry himself. Perhaps surprisingly, there has been relatively little discussion of there being a homoerotic, homosexual (or even homophobic) subtext to the novel. Jed's love for Joe could clearly have erotic overtones, but critics seem reluctant to explore these. The exception to this are Michelle Roberts who, in her review in *The Times* suggests that Jed represses his homosexuality while Joe denies that he has any such urges. Harvey Porlock, in a piece for the *Sunday Times*, takes issue with another critic, Philip Hensher, for objecting to McEwan's apparent association of homosexuality and psychosis. In a further twist to this particular strand of the novel, Christina Bynes, whose work on McEwan will be discussed later, quotes McEwan talking of a "back story" he invented for the two fake psychologists, Wenn and Camia, who purport to be the author of the paper with which the novel ends and whose names derive from McEwan's own:

they are a couple of homosexuals, who are only interested in homoerotic behaviour. If you look at their other published paper, it is called Homosexual erotomania, and was published in *Acta Psychiatrica Scandinavica*, which is a real journal and the most obscure that I could find (2002: p. 267)

It's probably most fruitful when interpreting the novel to see the homoerotic subtext as an aspect of its representation of masculinity in crisis. After all, Joe reveals himself early on in the novel to be insecure about his own body—when thinking about his relationship to the "beautiful" Clarissa, he describes himself as "a large, clumsy, balding fellow who could hardly believe his luck" (p. 7) and this is an uncertainty that Jed's avowal of love destabilizes even further.

Joe's narrative voice dominates throughout—even to the point of him narrating from Clarissa's point of view in Chapter Nine and referring to himself at this point in the third person. Both Clarissa's and Jed's voices only emerge unmediated by Joe's narrative in the letters they write to him (her name hints at this mode of narration, referring as it does to the greatest and longest of all epistolary novels). Mars-Jones expresses some dissatisfaction with Clarissa's role in the novel, suggesting that "for all her grounded emotions and insights, she has a lower status than, say, Julie in *The Child in Time*. McEwan's emotional engagement with feminism is less deferent than once it was" (1997: p. 16). This apparent downgrading of the feminized perspective could also be seen in the portrayal of Jed's character. Both his appearance (he has a ponytail), and his passionate, if unbalanced, commitment to the emotional and the intuitive, associate him with a view of knowledge that contrasts with the conventionally rationalist, masculine viewpoint as embodied in Joe, although the certainty of "knowing" that he displays mirrors Joe's in many ways. David Malcolm suggests that McEwan's "valuation of the men's and women's ways of seeing the world" is not the same as it is in *Or Shall we Die*, *The Child in Time*, or *Black Dogs*.

The prevalence of Joe's voice might be seen as a replication and confirmation of a dominant patriarchal discourse and some feminist critics of his work have also found an absence of "authentic" characterization in his female characters (Rogers: 1996). The literary echoes inscribed in Clarissa's name not only evoke the early epistolary form of the novel but also the female character's status as victim of male patriarchal aggression as Samuel Richardson's eighteenth-century heroine is stalked and pursued by the rapacious Squire B. In *Enduring Love*, McEwan complicates in a number of ways this pattern of privileged masculinity submerging the female. Clarissa is clearly associated with an intellectual humanism and literary sensibility that might be close to McEwan's own heart. She is also a scholar, researching the Romantic poet John Keats (1795–1821) and his relationship to Fanny Brawne, one of the most enduring love stories in English literature expressed for later readers largely through the letters sent between them (echoed in the letters that we are told Joe and Clarissa have exchanged early in their relationship and parodied in Jed's "love letters" to Joe that appear in the novel). The fact that Keats's poetry is sometimes associated with a feminized masculinity that celebrates beauty and its relationship to knowledge and truth adds to the blurring and disturbing of gender assumptions that the novel effects. Keatsian Romanticism may be associated with a philosophical tradition that prioritizes the heart over the mind, feelings over rationality.

Indeed, McEwan has said in a recent interview with Jonathan Noakes that he wanted the reader to side with Clarissa, to share her doubts about Joe's obsession with Jed Parry and to draw similarly erroneous conclusions from the various false trails that the "detective" or hermeneutic mode within novel sets in motion. "These are the games one plays, and withholding information is crucial to this kind of writing. But I wanted Clarissa to be wrong. I wanted the police to be wrong. I rather like those plots" (2002: p. 17).

In the same interview, he speaks of his desire to write a novel that "rather celebrated the rational" with a central male narrator who was "slightly repellent, but right." It's instructive to match the author's comments here with the conclusions drawn in Jago Morrison's article in the literary journal *Critique* (Spring 2001) which employs a range of interpretative approaches drawn from the work of literary theorists and writers such as Umberto Eco, Paul Ricoeur and Julia Kristeva to unpack gender and narrative in his later fiction.

Morrison sees *Enduring Love* as a novel about unease and insecurity in both the act of narration and in "the constitution of a moneyed, successful masculinity" (Morrison, 2001: p. 254). In this reading of the novel, Joe may be somewhat repellent and right but this masculine rectitude and security is seen to be under siege, stalked by the disruptive and irrational. For Morrison, Parry's threat to Joe's apparently secure rationality acts as a kind of catalyst for the revelation of an underlying insecurity that is already partially apparent in his uncertainty about the direction of his own career. (Joe feels himself to be excluded from the apparent safe objective world of academic scientific research to which he desires to return and has to negotiate with the messier, less predictable world of popular scientific journalism.) Morrison sees this unease as resulting in a "scrabbling for security" that Joe is continually denied as he attempts to line up the law and eventually the weight of psychiatry itself on his side. Hence the novel is crucially concerned with an "embattled masculinity" trying (and failing) to shore the privileged status of the male subject by invoking as defense "the public narratives of science, medicine and law" (Morrison, 2001: p. 254).

One of the most convincing elements in Morrison's reading of the novel is his point that the act of narration itself is a crucial part of this desire for control, as Joe attempts to use narrative as therapy to overcome the horror of the balloon accident and, more particularly to place the disruptive, intrusive and anarchic Jed within the comforting scientific narrative of De Clérambaut's syndrome, from which he gains much reassurance. "A syndrome was a framework of prediction and it offered a kind of comfort" (p. 124). Joe's desire to narrate "hammering the unspeakable into forms of words, threading single perceptions into narrative" (p. 30) is contrasted with Clarissa's desire to repeat, meditate on and hence confront, the very moment of Logan's horrific fall to the ground. The language that McEwan has Joe use here is significant, the "hammering" representing an apparently masculine desire to control and shape experience, if necessary by force. It's a characteristic gesture on Joe's part as he delights in the apparent power that words give him. McEwan clearly wants us to enjoy, albeit in retrospect, the ironically coalescing moments immediately after the accident when Joe and Jed exchange a look that catalyzes the disruption of Joe's life whereupon Joe immediately grasps the reassuringly solid "dense little slab" of his mobile phone to take control: "I was in the world, equipped, capable, connected" (p. 20).

Later in his essay, Morrison makes use of the work of the feminist writer Julia Kristeva, in particular her contrast between "intuition, mystical vision, and female subjectivity on the one hand and 'male-stream' linearity on the other—an opposition she finds in need of significant re-negotiation" (Morrison, 2001: p. 254). Joe's need to fix experience within the temporally linear mode of narration is here seen as an act of male repression as opposed to Clarissa's atemporal and non-linear focus on a particular image. (Perhaps an important modification to this gendered view of narrative is the fact that McEwan shows in Jean Logan's ultimately mistaken desire to construct a narrative around her husband's death that speaks of infidelity—a love that has not endured—and that such impulses may not solely be a product of gender. This is, of course, another of McEwan's false trails with which to trick the unwary reader.)

As we have already seen, the first of the appendices appears to offer a scholarly and detached account of the disruptive Jed that secures him firmly with the invisible bars of psychiatric discourse, just as he is bodily secured with the tangible walls of the psychiatric institution. But, of course, the article is completely fake — "an overdetermined gesture of legitimation," as Morrison calls it. So once again the reassuring (masculine) discourse of science and rationality is called into question, an effect redoubled by the fact that the very final voice in the novel is Jed's, and not Joe's, with its passionate assertion of "our love" which continues to endure in Jed's clearly disturbed mind. This inevitably denies us a fully comforting sense of closure, disrupting the usual hermeneutic code of the conventional detective novel where truth is revealed and order re-established.

Endings—The Child, Time, Knowledge

However, the novel doesn't leave the reader in a completely postmodern state of suspension and doubt since the actual end of the novel, of Joe's narrative, does offer some sense of restored and renewed equilibrium after the disruptive trauma that the accident and Jed have introduced into the characters' lives. It's important to note that the end is associated with the image of childhood, as the final exchanges involve John Logan's children in conversation with Joe.

As we have seen, childhood is a recurrent aspect of McEwan's work and some critics noticed its apparent absence from *Enduring Love*. But children are not entirely absent from the story. Indeed, Logan's children feature in the background and become an important symbol of renewal at the end. It is also important to remember that it is a child drifting in the out-of-control balloon that Joe and the others are trying to protect and save. Adam Mars-Jones notes in his review how unusual it is for McEwan to have a childless couple at the heart of a novel "so central did parenthood seem to his idea of human completeness" (1997: p. 16). The novel does seem to offer a kind of parody family in the triangular relationship between the three central figures—Clarissa calls Joe a child at one point, Jed seems to be both would-be lover and also a kind of surrogate son to Joe as well as representing an alter ego that is reflected in the closeness of their Christian names.

But families in this novel are associated with conflict and pain rather than cohesion. Apart from Clarissa's own inability to conceive and the fact that her father has suffered from Alzheimer's disease, the Logan family has to deal with sudden death and lingering suspicion and Clarissa's brother Luke's fifteen-year-long marriage is, we are told in Chapter 5, in an echo of the novel's dominant image, "falling apart."

Literary images of childhood aren't far away, either, as the scene is taking place in Oxford "on the river bank where Lewis Carroll, the Dean of Christ Church, had once entertained the darling objects of his own obsessions" (p. 230). Carroll's obsessions, of course, gave us two of the greatest works of children's literature—rather more productive than Jed Parry's—but the Alice reference suggests more about the world of childhood as a location where adults can perhaps discover themselves anew. (Oddly Joe gets his facts wrong here— Carroll was never Dean of Christ Church, but Alice Liddell was the daughter of the Dean, a sign, perhaps, of a productive fallibility in his hitherto confidently factual approach to the world.)

The other Carroll reference in the novel, when Joe compares Johnny B. Well to the dormouse at the Mad Hatter's tea party, underlines the novel's dominant sense of how easy it is to step out of one apparently sane, rational world into one characterized by chaos and ultimately madness. The end of Joe's narrative seems to offer this kind of redemptive possibility, as Joe's much vaunted "talent for clarity" (p. 75) is now put at the service not of a rather mechanical production process of scientific journalism but about "that thing about the river"—a genuine engagement with a child's desire to know, in this case about water and rivers with all their symbolic associations of life, time and rebirth.

To overstress this aspect of the ending would be to sentimentalize and that is not a word in McEwan's vocabulary. But the certainly positive group image with which the novel ends—Joe with the two children at either side of him—is an obvious reworking of the image of failed group cohesion with which it opened.

Most important of all is Joe's acknowledgement of not knowing (about his and Clarissa's future) that appears in the final paragraphs—a kind of unconscious acknowledgement of the importance of positive doubt, referring obliquely perhaps to the Keatsian notion of Negative Capability. Keats coined the phrase "Negative Capability" in a letter written to his brothers George and Thomas on December 21, 1817. In this letter he defined his concept thus: "I mean Negative Capability, that is when man is capable of being in uncertainties, mysteries, doubts, without any irritable reaching after fact and reason." It is this state of productive uncertainty that McEwan seems to celebrate, or at least acknowledge, in Joe's state of mind at the end of the novel.

Summing Up the Novel

The most substantial discussions of *Enduring Love*, since the first reviews, have appeared in two recent studies of McEwan's writing, both of which were published in 2002. Reference has already been made to David Malcolm who, in his monograph on the author *Understanding Ian McEwan* (2002), devotes a chapter entitled "Science and Fictions" to a detailed discussion of the novel's major themes. Malcolm sees McEwan's sixth novel as confirming his status as "a very substantial writer" and focuses his analysis on the novel's exploration of the fragility of love, its concern with epistemological doubt and the limitations of knowledge, and the self-aware ways in which McEwan draws the reader's attention to the book's status as narrative. Initially in his discussion, Malcolm points to what he judges to be the "deeply traditional" nature of narrative in *Enduring Love*, describing it as "a traditional and accessible novel without any substantial degree of experimentation in terms of narrative and narration." Malcolm stresses the degree to which it is a psychological study, predominantly of one man, Joe, "an analysis of a complex individual." The implications for the narrative structure of the novel are clear: "A substantially reliable first-person narrator gives an account of events. The utterances of other characters are largely contained within this character's narration and are under his control" (Malcolm, 2002: p. 160). But *control* is, of course, a key word in the novel right from the very opening as Joe and the others attempt to handle the balloon; the desire for control, and its illusory nature is something that comes to haunt all the main characters in one way or another. In the later stages of his discussion of the novel, Malcolm somewhat revises this view of *Enduring Love* as a predominantly conventional story by pointing to its moments of self-consciousness, when Joe reminds us that he himself is telling a story. This aspect of the novel was first commented upon by Oliver Reynolds in a review in the *Times Literary Supplement* in which he points to a number of sentences that "proclaim a self-aware narrative, a story as experiment, one where the telling will distance us from what is told" (Malcolm: 2002, p. 179). So perhaps, as Malcolm tacitly acknowledges, the surface conventionality disguises a more questioning meditation on the slipperiness of knowledge and the necessarily partial, fictive nature of storytelling.

Perhaps the most revealing part of Malcolm's study of the novel is his view of Joe as "the picture of a man driven by guilt"—guilt

which pursues him throughout the novel and which stems mainly
from his letting go of the rope and the subsequent death of Logan.
Although Malcolm doesn't follow this through to consider the idea
of a masculinity in crisis, he does relate Joe's increasing self-doubt
to what he calls "a deep existential upheaval" which sees Joe fall out
of his supposedly secure world of science and love for Clarissa and
into a nightmare of madness and obsession created by Jed Parry. The
echoes of Lewis Carroll's *Alice in Wonderland* are curiously present
here too as Joe reflects on this dramatic change: "It was as if I had
fallen through a crack in my own existence, down into another life,
another set of sexual preferences, another past history and future"
(p. 67). Jed turns out to be as mad as a Hatter, but with rather more
realistically violent consequences than in Wonderland. Again, like
Alice, Joe attempts to hang on to facts in an increasingly unstable
environment, in this case the "hundred feet or so of box-files" and "the
little skyscraper of a hard disk drive" that provide him with his archive
of knowledge and the materialist, empirical data on which he bases
his worldview. Malcolm rightly stresses the provisional nature of this
knowledge suggesting that ". . . what the novel also shows is that knowledge is (like love) a rather fragile thing, difficult to get and, indeed,
rather unstable. An atmosphere of epistemological uncertainty be-
devils the world of *Enduring Love*" (Malcolm, 2002: p. 177).

One final point that emerges from Malcolm's account, and
which few other commentators on the novel note, is the relative lack
of any socio-historical context for the novel's action. The social setting he describes as "very homogeneous. Apart from excursions to
police stations, the world is that of libraries, radio producers, univer-
sities, good restaurants and expensive apartments" (Malcolm, 2002:
p. 171). Even Joe's brief encounter with the "criminal" world only
leads to somewhat deranged ex-hippies who are described by Johnny
B. Well as "intellectuals." There are relatively few clues as to the
time in which the novel is set—a vaguely 1990s milieu which can

be calculated from the fact that the two hundredth anniversary of Keats's birth is imminent, which sets the novel just before 1995. Similarly, the characters' own pasts are only sketchily drawn, all of which tends to accentuate the claustrophic psychological emphasis of the narrative, intensifying its focus on the individual consciousness as it grapples with experience. Malcolm sees this as McEwan's return to the "eerily insulated" worlds of *The Cement Garden* and *The Comfort of Strangers* after McEwan's excursion into the more socially and historically rooted worlds of the novels that immediately preceded the novel in question. This may be true up to a point, but *Enduring Love* lacks the more gothic excesses of McEwan's earlier fiction and locates itself very firmly in the intellectual climate of the *fin de siècle*, in particular the broadening of the boundaries of science and the popularizing of theory through the work of Richard Dawkins and Stephen Hawking, among others.

McEwan's fascination with contemporary scientific theories is dealt with extensively in the other recent study of the novel that forms part of a major account of his work. This is perhaps not surprising since the author, Christina Byrnes, herself draws heavily on psychological approaches, in particular the work of C. J. Jung— hence the title of her study, *The Work of Ian McEwan—a psychodynamic approach* (2002). Byrnes draws strong parallels between McEwan's and Joe's views on the relationship between science, in particular biology and genetics, and human moral dilemmas. She cites McEwan's extensive writing on the topic in newspaper articles and links his ideas with those of E. O. Wilson, from whose work Joe quotes in Chapter Nine. It's an important moment in the novel that has already been noted, and it clearly defines the differing attitudes that Clarissa and Joe have toward human nature and love—Joe espouses that new, neo-Darwinian orthodoxy of evolutionary and genetic determinism which Clarissa rejects as a "new fundamentalism," a revealing remark that suggests the paradoxical links between Joe's and Jed's positions:

Twenty years ago you and your friends were all socialists and you blamed the environment for everyone's hard luck. Now you've got us trapped in our genes and there's a reason for everything!" She was perturbed when I read Wilson's passage to her. Everything was being stripped down, she said, and in the process some larger meaning was lost (p. 70).

It's also significant that the subject they have been discussing is the effect of a baby's smile—another link to the novel's recurrent image of childhood. Of course Joe (like McEwan) is fully aware that scientific thinking goes in fashions—chaos theory out, new evolutionary theory in—and the novel draws on both, showing the chaotic nature of experience as well as the conflicted relationship between science and religion in the ongoing debate on human origins and the existence of God. Byrnes perhaps misses the fact that, while attracted to the New Science, McEwan fully acknowledges the human need for mystery—Clarissa may be wrong about Jed Parry, but her philosophical and emotional standpoint is given due weight and meaning as suggested in the previous chapter. McEwan has suggested that in exploring this debate ". . . I'm continuing a conversation I had with myself in another novel, *Black Dogs*" (*Capitola* Interview, 1998: p. 3), and it's a conversation that has clearly not come to an end.

A more controversial aspect of Byrnes's study is her linking of the novel's central character not only with McEwan's interest in science but also with details from his personal biography. The ending of McEwan's marriage to Penny Allen preceded the writing of the novel and the conflict that resulted from the divorce was ongoing until 1998, by which time McEwan had remarried. Byrnes identifies a link with the subject matter of the novel here—the various marital stresses that permeate the narrative in the foreground (Joe and Clarissa) but also in the background (Clarissa's brother, Jean Logan's belief that her husband was having an affair with a younger woman, the actual affair between Bonnie Deedes and the older James Reid, Professor of Logic—a nice McEwanesque touch of irony here). In a somewhat bald statement, Byrnes suggests that "Joe shares McEwan's mid-life identity crisis" (p. 260) and throughout her account of the novel suggests that the personal identification between author and character is stronger than in any other of the novels. Continuing this line of interpretation, Byrnes suggests that:

It is part of the mid-life crisis to re-evaluate the ideas and ideals of one's youth in the light of experience. *Enduring Love* leaves the reader with an impression of disappointment and loss of faith in goodness, morality and any kind of spiritual values. There is humour in the description of what became of the hippies of the late 60s and 70s. It is hard to imagine that McEwan had once belonged with this group, wore his hair long, took drugs and drove a bus to Kabul (Byrnes, 2002: p. 254).

Whether or not it is helpful for the reader to make connections between Joe and McEwan (and biography can often be an unreliable starting point for interpretation) this seems to give a rather bleak assessment of the novel's position on moral, scientific and spiritual matters, which surely end on a more productively ambiguous note, with indications of emotional reconciliation and an acknowledgement of a potential shift in Joe's apparently rigid rationality.

Arguably the most enlightening section of Byrnes's discussion of the novel emerges, not surprisingly, from her psychological reference points. She employs a sustained Jungian approach throughout her study of McEwan's work which is at its most helpful in relation to *Enduring Love* when she uses Jung's notion of the "shadow" self—the dark, repressed other that is a necessary complement to the individual's identity—to explore the links between Joe and his "stalker" Jed:

Stalking or being stalked can be understood as the activity of the shadow and illustrates the impossibility of repressing unconscious material permanently. Neither is it possible to separated oneself from it for ever, by projecting it into someone else, because they will stalk or attract stalking behaviour in an effect to unite the self and the shadow in the service of wholeness (Byrnes, 2002: p. 263).

She goes on to suggest that: "The power struggle between them is like the contest between the ego and the shadow, described repeatedly in mythology as the theme of the 'hostile brethren'" (p. 269). There are, of course, circumstantial similarities between these two seeming opposites—Clarissa notices the similarities between their handwriting and wonders for a while whether Jed exists, as she is never at home when the former makes his phone calls. That this is another of McEwan's false trails doesn't necessarily take away from the undefined sense of a close proximity between the men, as though Jed represents the darker, repressed "shadow" side of Joe's seemingly enlightened rationality—an increasingly hostile mirror-self that exposes the instability of the ego. Clarissa even talks about their relationship in clinical terms at one point, telling Joe that: "He's not the cause of your agitation, he's a symptom" (p. 84). A little later Joe remarks that "[She] considered Parry my fault. He was the kind of phantom that only I could have called up, a spirit of my dislocated, incomplete character . . ." (p. 102). Byrnes gives a more detailed account of De Clérambault's syndrome and its role in the novel than any other critic, reminding us of the reality of the psychiatric disorder and its place in the history of pathology. As can be deduced from the references cited in McEwan's fake essay on the subject in the appendix, all of which are apparently authentic except the last (by the fictional Wenn and Camia), there was a revival of interest in the subject in the late 1980s and 1990s due to the increased number of stalkers who were being publicly prosecuted. Byrnes reminds us that the representation of extreme mental states, including stalking, has occurred before in McEwan's work and is obviously part of his interest in the unlit, darker spaces of the human psyche. She also points out that Joe does little or nothing to help Jed: "He shows him no compassion and makes no effort to mobilise the medical or psychiatric services on his behalf" (p. 268). His actions are all designed to repress and ultimately silence Jed—a course of action in which he is only partially successful, as the novel's final pages reveal. In the end, Christina Byrnes's reading is certainly uneven at times, but undoubtedly performs a useful corrective to the construction of the novel as a battle of opposites as she envisages the two main protagonists as two sides of a conflicted whole, "hostile brethren" in an archetypal struggle between mind and feeling.

5

Further Reading and Discussion Questions

1. McEwan: "I came across a journal entry I wrote about six months after I began working on *Enduring Love* . . . [I]t said 'Write a first chapter that would be the equivalent of a highly addictive drug.' I did want to have the reader hit the ground running" (in interview with Eric Schoeck).

   How far would you agree that McEwan has made the first chapter particularly vivid and effective, striking or memorable? Comment on the details, methods, and/or techniques he has used.

2. "The beginning is simple to mark" (p. 1); "[a] beginning is an artifice" (p. 17). What do you think McEwan might be saying about the beginning of a story?

3. On p. 5, Joe thinks that ballooning is "a precarious form of transport when the wind, rather than the pilot, set the course. Then I thought that perhaps this was the very nature of its attraction." Why do you think it is a balloon accident, as opposed to an accident of some other kind, that McEwan has chosen?

4. "We were seven years into a childless marriage of love" (p. 8). How would you say the novel represents Joe and Clarissa's relationship?

5. Reread the description of the attempt to hold down the balloon on pages 13–14. McEwan has commented that "They know that if they can all hang on, their combined weight will bring the thing to the ground. If one lets go, it's crazy for anyone else to hang on. In this I saw a parable, a microcosm of one of those great conflicts in our lives between altruism and that other primary necessity of looking after yourself" (interview with Eric Schoeck). Think about how this scene presents this "great conflict." What might it be saying about the ways individuals relate to each other? How does this bear on the rest of the novel?

6. In Chapter 2, Joe says, "[I]t was a random matter, who was alive or dead at any given time" (p. 19). How does *Enduring Love* establish and explore the idea of the random?

7. When he is looking at Logan's body, Joe says, "I understood why a pre-scientific age would have needed to invent the soul" (p. 23). What would you say about Joe's attitude to religion, and, also, about his attitude to Jed at the end of this chapter, when he says, "I decided he ought to know the truth. 'Because, my friend, no one's listening. There's no one up there'" (p. 26)?

8. Joe tells us that in Clarissa's view, Logan's fall is "a challenge no angel could resist, and his death denied their existence" (p. 31). Why do you think Logan's death is so important to Clarissa and to Joe himself?

9. In the *Salon* interview, McEwan was asked about the tension in the novel between rationality and religious belief: "At one point a character says, 'rationality is a kind of innocence.' I'm wondering what you meant by that." McEwan responded, "With [Joe's] organized mind he can take things too literally. There is something about Clarissa's take on the world that Joe badly needs." How do you think the novel establishes the idea of different "takes" on the world, as McEwan puts it here?

10. How would you respond to the suggestion that the novel is about what Jago Morrison refers to as a crisis in "successful, moneyed masculinity?"

11. Consider the importance of other texts, writing and writers in *Enduring Love*. You might like to think about Clarissa's interest in Keats, her reference to Milton, McEwan's allusions to the thriller, Joe's interest in Darwin.

12. What do you think the novel seems to be saying about contemporary developments in science, or what Clarissa calls "the new fundamentalism?"

13. Discuss the ways in which characters in *Enduring Love* use storytelling as a way of making sense of what happens.

14. First-person narrative can only ever present one character's perspective on events. How does *Enduring Love* make use of this kind of narrative?

15. What do you think is the significance of Jed's particular mental condition and what effect does the inclusion of the appendices have on the way we understand the novel?

Select Bibliography

1. WORKS BY IAN McEWAN

First Love, Last Rites. London: Jonathan Cape, 1975. Short stories.

In Between the Sheets. London: Jonathan Cape, 1978. Short stories.

The Cement Garden. London: Jonathan Cape, 1978.

The Comfort of Strangers. London: Jonathan Cape, 1981.

The Imitation Game: Three Plays for Television. London: Jonathan Cape, 1981.

Or Shall We Die? Words for an Oratorio Set to Music by Michael Berkeley. London: Jonathan Cape, 1983.

The Ploughman's Lunch. London: Methuen, 1985. Screenplay.

Rose Blanche. Text by Ian McEwan. Pictures by Roberto Innocenti. Based on a story by Christopher Gallaz. London: Jonathan Cape, 1985. Picture book for children.

A Child in Time. London: Jonathan Cape, 1987.

Soursweet. London: Faber & Faber, 1988. Screenplay based on Timothy Mo's novel *Sour Sweet* (1982).

A Move Abroad: Or Shall We Die? and The Ploughman's Lunch. London: Pan Books, 1989.

The Innocent. London: Jonathan Cape, 1990.

Black Dogs. London: Jonathan Cape, 1992.

The Daydreamer. London: Jonathan Cape, 1994.
Enduring Love. London: Jonathan Cape, 1997.
Amsterdam. London: Jonathan Cape, 1998.
Atonement. London: Jonathan Cape, 2001.

Uncollected Short Stories:

"Intersection." in *TriQuarterly* (Fall 1975): pp. 63–86.
"Untitled." in *TriQuarterly* (Winter 1976): pp. 62–3.
"Deep Sleep, Light Sleeper." in *Harpers & Queen* (August 1977): pp. 82–5.

2. SELECTED REVIEWS AND ARTICLES ON *ENDURING LOVE*

Birkets, Sven. "Grand Delusion." *New York Times Book Review* January 25, 1998: p. 7.*

Brookner, Anita. "Desire and Pursuit." *The Spectator* August 30, 1997: pp. 28–9.

Connolly, Cressida. "Over-Fished Waters." *Literary Review.**

Craig, Amanda. "Out of the Balloon." *New Statesman* September 5, 1997: p. 43.

Dinnage, Rosemary. "So Alert with Love." *The New York Review of Books* April 9, 1998: pp. 32–33.*

Lehmann-Haupt, Christopher. "Science vs. the Divine, with Suspense and Passion." *New York Times* January 15, 1998: p. E11.

Mars-Jones, Adam. "I Think I'm Right, Therefore I Am." *The Observer Review* September 7, 1997: p. 16.*

Meyer, Harriet. JAMA: *the Journal of the American Medical Association* 279. 2 (June 1998).*

Morrison, Jago. "Narration and Unease in Ian McEwan's later fiction." *Critique* 42. 3 (Spring 2001): pp. 253–68.*

Reynolds Oliver. "A Master of Accidents." *Times Literary Supplement* September 12, 1997: p. 12.

Sayers, Valerie. *Commonweal* 125: 9 (May 8, 1998): pp. 24–6.*

Wood Michael. "When the Balloon Goes Up." *London Review of Books* September 4, 1997: pp. 8–9.

* these reviews are currently available on the Web

3. WEB MATERIALS

Bold Type: Interview with Ian McEwan,
www.randomhouse.com/boldtype/0398/mcewan/interview.html

British Council "Contemporary Writers: Ian McEwan,"
www.contemporarywriters.com/authors/

Connolly, Cressida. "Over-fished Waters," *Literary Review,*
www.users.dircon.co.uk/~litrev/199709/Connolly.html

Ian McEwan Website,
www.ianmcewan.ws/bib/books/enduring.html
The most extensive online source of materials on McEwan

Gardner, Dwight. An Interview with Ian McEwan *Salon,*
www.salonmagazine.com/books/int/1998/03/cov-si-3/nt.html

Judd Elizabeth, Review of *Enduring Love: Salon,*
archive.salon.com/books/sneaks/1998/02/20review.html

Miller Laura, "Ian McEwan fools British shrinks," *Salon,*
www.salon.com/books/log/1999/09/21/mcewan/print.html

Schoek, Eric An Interview with Ian McEwan, *Capitola Book Café,*
www.capitolabookcafé.com/andrea/mcewan.html

Whitney, Helen, "Frontline Interview with Ian McEwan,"
www.pbs.org/wgbh/pages/frontline/shows/faith/interviews/mcewan.html
Specifically focuses on the events of 11 September

4. INTERVIEWS

Begley, Adam. "The Art of Fiction CLXXIII." *The Paris Review* 162 (Summer, 2002).*

Billen, Andrew. "Eng Lit's leading expert on evil." *Evening Standard* September 26, 2001: pp. 27–8.

Gonzalez, Rosa. "The Pleasure of Prose Writing versus Pornographic Violence: An Interview with Ian McEwan." *Barcelona English Language*

* currently available on the Web

and Literature Studies, 3 (1999): pp. 55–62. Also in *The European English Messenger* 1.3 (Autumn, 1992): pp. 40–5.

Haffenden, John. *Novelists in Interview.* London: Methuen, 1985: pp. 168–90.

Hamilton, Ian. "Points of Departure." *New Review* 5.2 (Autumn, 1978): pp. 9–21.

Hunt, Adam. "Ian McEwan." *New Fiction* 21 (Winter, 1996): pp. 47–50.

Kellaway, Kate. "At home with his worries." *The Observer Review* September 16, 2001.*

Ricks, Christopher. "Adolescence and After." *The Listener* April 12, 1979: pp. 526–7.

5. VIDEO AND AUDIO

Writers Talk: Ideas of Our Time, Guardian Conversations 69. Institute of Contemporary Arts. Ian McEwan in conversation with Martin Amis. On *The Child in Time.*

Lawson, Mark. "The Ian McEwan Interview." *Front Row BBC* Radio 4, December 2001 (producer Ekene Akalawu).

6. GENERAL BIOGRAPHICAL AND CRITICAL STUDIES

Byrnes, Christina. *The Work of Ian McEwan: a psychodynamic approach.* Nottingham: Pauper's Press, 2002, pp. 248–271 on *Enduring Love.*

Cochran, Angus B. "Ian McEwan (1948–   )," in George Stade (ed.), *British Writers. Supplement IV.* New York: Scribner's, 1997, pp. 389–408.

Cowley, Jason. "Portrait: Ian McEwan." *Prospect* (December 1998): pp. 42–45.

Fletcher, John. "Ian McEwan." *Dictionary of Literary Biography 14. British Novelists Since 1960, Part 2: H-Z.* Detroit: Gale, 1983: pp. 495–500.

Grant, Damian and Ian McEwan. *Contemporary Writers: Ian McEwan.* London: The Book Trust and the British Council, 1989.

* currently available on the Web

Lewis, Peter. "Ian McEwan," in *Contemporary Novelists ed.* Lesley Henderson, 5th edition London and Chicago: St James Press, 1991: pp. 621–3.

McEwan, Ian. "Mother Tongue: a memoir." *The Guardian* October 13, 2001.

———. "Only Childhood: Ian McEwan Remembers Growing up Without Brothers and Sisters," *Observer* January 31, 1982: p. 41.

Malcolm, David. *Understanding Ian McEwan.* Columbia: University of South Carolina Press, 2002, pp. 155–181 on *Enduring Love.*

Mars-Jones, Adam. *Venus Envy. Chatto Counterblasts no.14.* London: Chatto & Windus, 1990.

Massie, Allan. *The Novel Today: A Critical Guide to the British Novel 1970–1989.* London: Longman, 1990.

Reynolds, Margaret and Jonathan Noakes. *Ian McEwan: The Essential Guide.* London: Vintage, 2002, pp. 81–123 on *Enduring Love.* Includes recent interview with McEwan and study activities on the novel.

Ryan, Kiernan. *Ian McEwan.* Plymouth: Northcote-House Publishers, 1994.

Slay, Jack Jr. *Ian McEwan.* New York: Twayne Publishers, 1996.

Taylor, D.J. "Ian McEwan: Standing up for the Sisters," in *A Vain Conceit: British Fiction in the 1980s.* London: Bloomsbury, 1989.

7. OTHER WORKS CITED

Hutcheon, Linda. *The Poetics of Postmodernism: History, Theory, Fiction.* London and New York: Routledge, 1998.

Lyotard, Jean-François. *The Postmodern Condition: A Report on Knowledge,* translated by Geoff Bennington and Brian Massumi, Manchester University Press 1984. Originally published 1979.

McHale, Brian. *Constructing Postmodernism.* London and New York: Routledge, 1992.

Midgley, Mary. "Why you can't lose with Darwin," *The Guardian* letters, February 8, 1998.

Money, John. *Love and Love Stories: the Science of Sex, Gender Difference and Pair Bonding.* Baltimore: Johns Hopkins University Press, 1981.

Radford, Tim. "And Darwin Created Us All," *The Guardian*, February 6, 1998.

Rorty, Richard. "Philosophers, Novelists and Inter-Cultural Comparison: Heidegger, Kundera and Dickens," paper presented to the Sixth East-West Philosophers' Conference, Honolulu, July 31–August 11, 1989.